Instructional Fair's *Addition and Subtraction — Grade 3* is the perfect way for students to learn about addition and subtraction of whole numbers! The format of this book allows your students to have a great time as they learn important skills/concepts dealing with addition and subtraction.

All of the skills/concepts presented include a teaching page which introduces and explains the material. Step-by-step instructions are also provided on this page and serve to further simplify the skill/concept.

Opposite each teaching page is a fun and exciting puzzle, game or other activity students can complete to practice the skill/concept. These activities help students understand how addition and subtraction are not only fun but are important and relevant aspects of mathematics as well.

To help students fully understand how addition and subtraction influence many aspects of their daily lives, present them with situations in which addition and subtraction are used. See if they can come up with other situations in which these skills are used. All of this will make students' learning seem much more relevant.

Ideally, these skills/concepts will be taught in the classroom or at home by a parent or tutor where manipulatives are available if necessary. Some students need concrete objects to fully grasp a new skill/concept.

An Answer Key is provided on pages 44-48 so that you or the students can check their work. This is also a great tool to use to check students' comprehension and any other strengths or weaknesses.

So, let Instructional Fair help your students have fun learning the very important mathematical concepts of addition and subtraction with this easy-to-use Basic Skills book.

Addition — Regrouping Ones

This high-rise needs a real mathematician to clean all of its windows! And, that's you!

1. Add ones. Ask: Do I need to regroup?

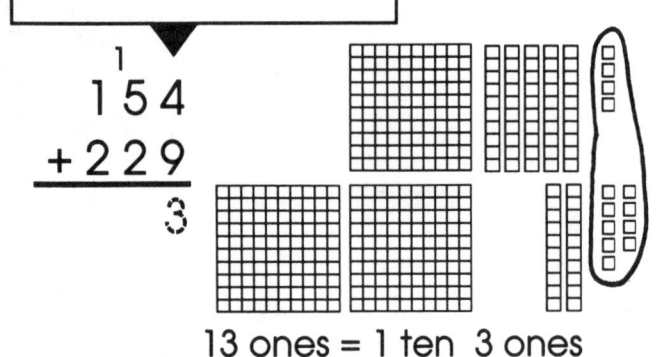

$$\begin{array}{r} \overset{1}{1}54 \\ +229 \\ \hline 3 \end{array}$$

13 ones = 1 ten 3 ones

2. Add tens. Ask: Do I need to regroup?

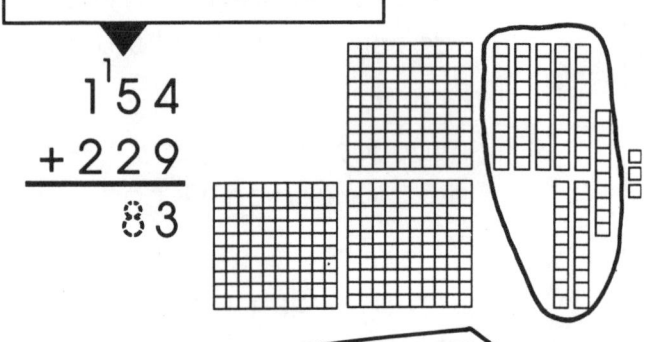

$$\begin{array}{r} \overset{1}{1}54 \\ +229 \\ \hline 83 \end{array}$$

3. Add hundreds.

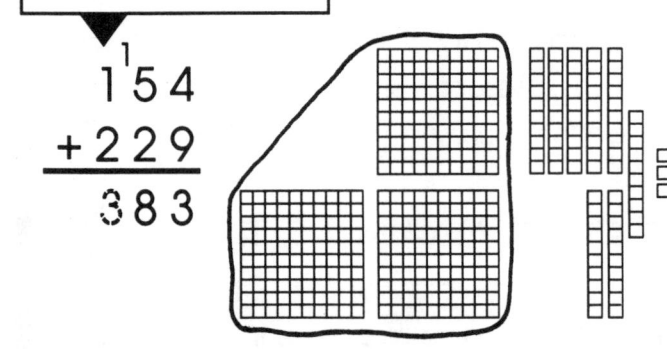

$$\begin{array}{r} \overset{1}{1}54 \\ +229 \\ \hline 383 \end{array}$$

383 windows in all!

Add. Regroup when needed.

$$\begin{array}{r} 406 \\ +248 \\ \hline \end{array} \qquad \begin{array}{r} 829 \\ +168 \\ \hline \end{array} \qquad \begin{array}{r} 928 \\ +54 \\ \hline \end{array}$$

$$\begin{array}{r} 643 \\ +254 \\ \hline \end{array} \qquad \begin{array}{r} 425 \\ +248 \\ \hline \end{array} \qquad \begin{array}{r} 306 \\ +429 \\ \hline \end{array}$$

Math IF5104

©MCMXCIV Instructional Fair, Inc.

Addition Ace

Addition — Regrouping Ones

Add. The pilot will remain in the air for as long as it takes to complete these problems.

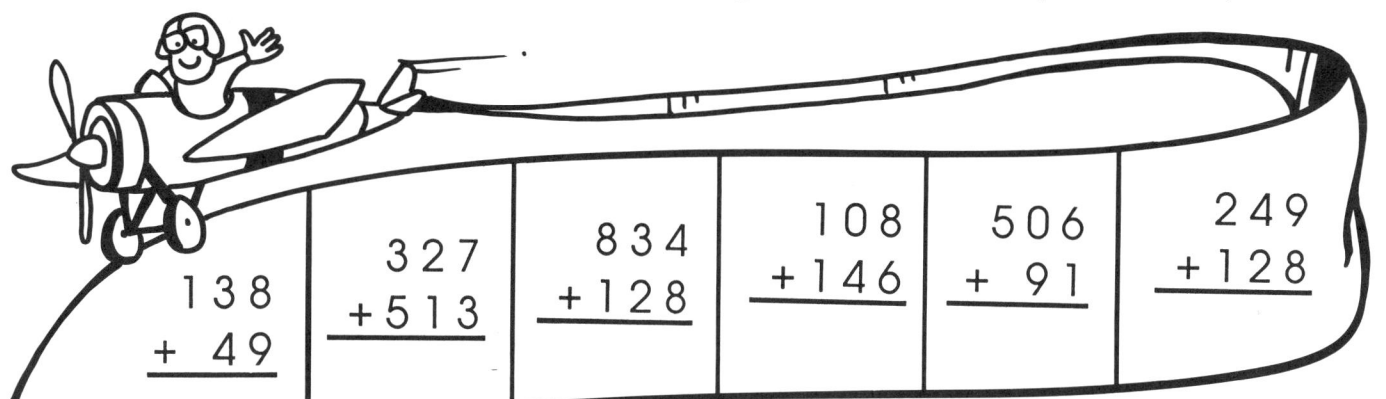

```
 138      327      834      108      506      249
+ 49     +513     +128     +146     + 91     +128
```

Color the ribbon if the sum is in the:

- 100's = green
- 200's = yellow
- 300's = red
- 400's = blue
- 500's = purple
- 600's = orange
- 700's = pink
- 800's = gold
- 900's = silver

```
 367      724      704      691      265
+424     + 39     +283     +205     +319
```

```
 432      528      924      306      226
+249     +349     + 56     +248     +165
```

```
 826      328      426      747
+164     +145     +261     +143
```

Addition — Regrouping Tens

Learn-a-Lot Elementary
Pet Owner Survey
Results: 425 students own dogs.
192 students own cats.

What is the total number of dogs and cats owned by students at Learn-a-Lot Elementary School?

1. Add ones. Ask: Do I need to regroup?

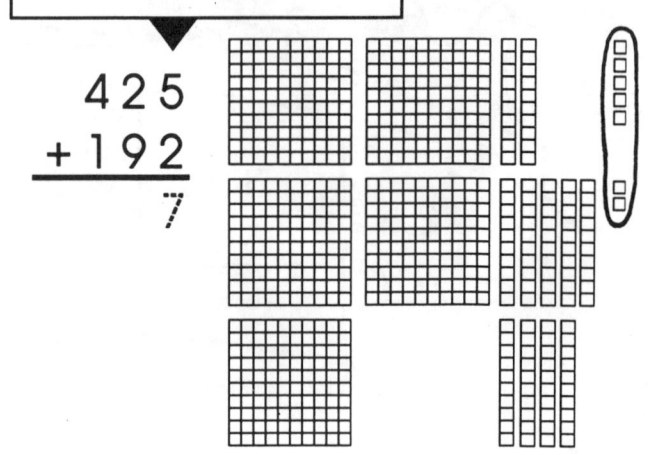

   ```
     4 2 5
   + 1 9 2
   ─────────
         7
   ```

2. Add tens. Ask: Do I need to regroup?

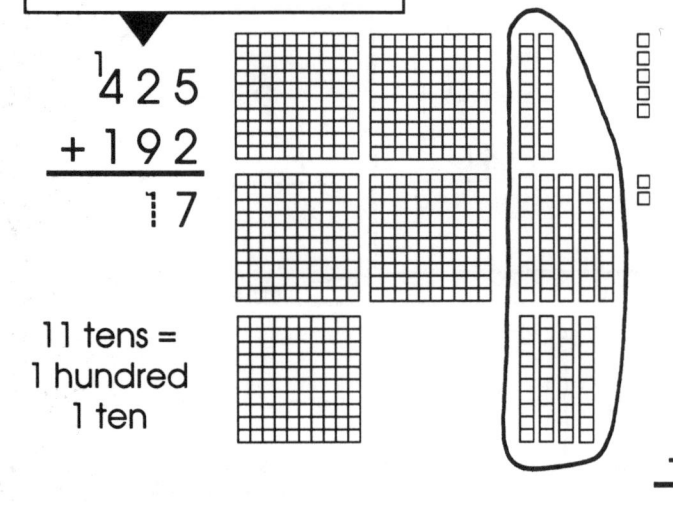

   ```
     ¹4 2 5
   + 1 9 2
   ─────────
       1 7
   ```

   11 tens =
   1 hundred
   1 ten

3. Add hundreds.

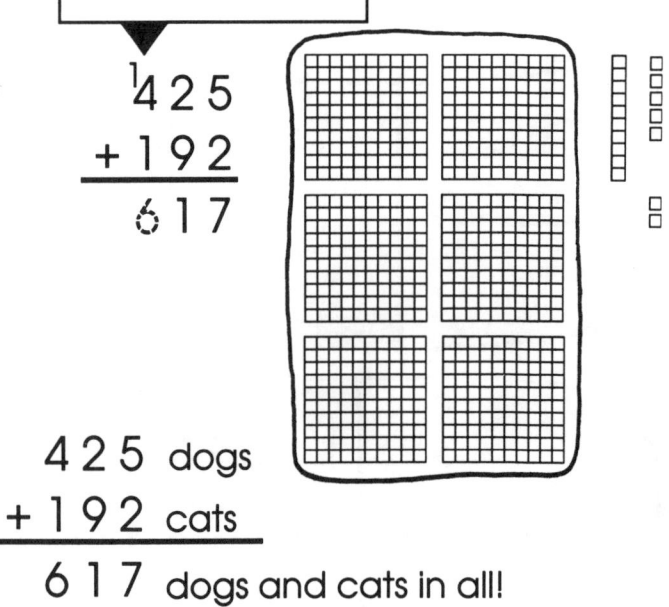

   ```
     ¹4 2 5
   + 1 9 2
   ─────────
     6 1 7
   ```

   4 2 5 dogs
   + 1 9 2 cats
   ─────────────
   6 1 7 dogs and cats in all!

Add. Regroup when needed.

```
  475        389        427
+ 252      + 234      + 196


  736        628        846
+ 191      + 191      + 188
```

I Want . . .

Addition — Regrouping Tens

Learn-a-Lot Elementary Wish List

Survey: How many children want to own these types of pets?

Dogs:

   4 5 6 want Dalmatians
 + 2 8 1 want Great Danes

Guinea Pigs:

   7 6 4 want black ones
 + 1 9 2 want any color

Kittens:

   2 4 6 want Siamese
 + 5 9 2 want Persians

Rabbits:

   3 5 6 want cottontails
 + 5 4 8 want angoras

Horses:

   2 3 8 want Shetland ponies
 + 3 8 4 want pintos

Toy Dogs:

   4 8 9 want toy spaniels
 + 2 4 6 want toy Chihuahuas

Lizards:

   6 5 2 want chameleons
 + 2 8 9 want iguanas

Birds:

   3 8 6 want parrots
 + 2 9 3 want parakeets

Fish:

   7 6 5 want neon tetras
 + 2 1 9 want goldfish

Snakes:

   2 6 3 want bull snakes
 + 4 8 5 want king snakes

Gerbils or Mice:

   8 4 3 want gerbils
 + 1 2 2 want mice

Pigs:

   3 4 0 want spotted swine
 + 2 9 8 want American
          landraces

Addition — Regrouping Tens

Astronaut Timmy Starbright trained 362 days the first year. The second year, he trained 275 days. How many days did he train his first two years?

13 tens = 1 hundred 3 tens

1. Add ones. Ask: Do I need to regroup?

```
  362
+ 275
─────
    7
```

2. Add tens. Ask: Do I need to regroup?

```
 ¹362
+ 275
─────
   37
```

3. Add hundreds.

```
 ¹362
+ 275
─────
  637
```

Timmy trained a total of 637 days his first two years of astronaut training.

```
  362   first year
+ 275   second year
─────
  637   total for 2 years
```

Add. Regroup when needed.

```
  281        346          362
+ 426      + 172        + 281

              534          529          472
            + 293        + 190        + 283
```

Space Shuttle Addition

Addition — Regrouping Tens

Experience addition in space as the payload specialist under zero gravity conditions.

```
  371        629        146
+ 439      + 184      + 587

  264        438        347
+ 483      + 290      + 328

  362        528        382
+ 459      + 391      + 249

  327        283        409
+ 649      + 346      + 292

  465        566        283
+ 193      + 283      + 519

  423        625        498
+ 392      + 246      + 123
```

Addition — Regrouping Hundreds

1. Add ones. Ask: Do I need to regroup?

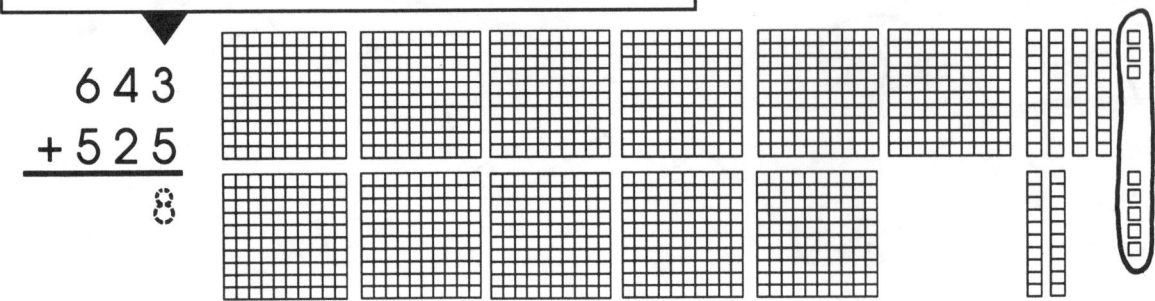

   6 4 3
   + 5 2 5
   ———
   8

2. Add tens. Ask: Do I need to regroup?

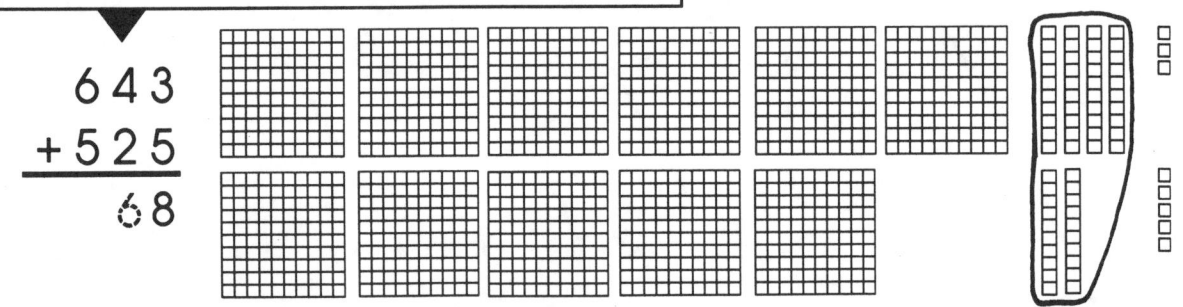

   6 4 3
   + 5 2 5
   ———
   6 8

3. Add hundreds. Ask: Do I need to regroup?

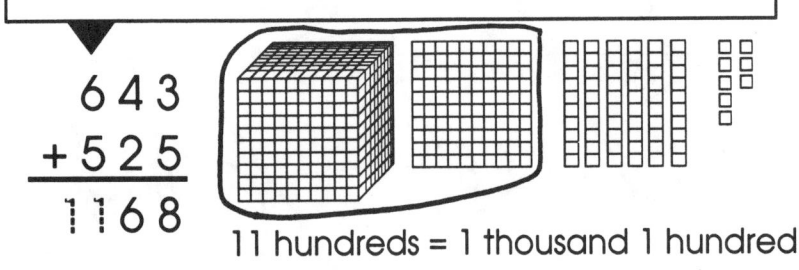

   6 4 3
   + 5 2 5
   ———
   1 1 6 8

   11 hundreds = 1 thousand 1 hundred

Add. Regroup when needed.

   9 4 2   5 6 4   4 7 3
   + 8 3 7   + 7 2 5   + 6 1 9

         6 2 0   3 8 5   3 0 8
         + 8 3 9   + 2 6 1   + 9 2 4

Let's Climb to the Top!

Addition — Regrouping Hundreds

```
    921      409      328
  + 87     +736     +449

562
+614

  824      246      982      207
 +597     +492     +220     +913

                              621
                             +489

           547      462      826
          +782     +781     + 95
284
+493
           429      506
          +636     +214     200
                           +489

                              684
                             +519
           623      536      425
          +192     +184     +594
```

Addition — Regrouping Hundreds

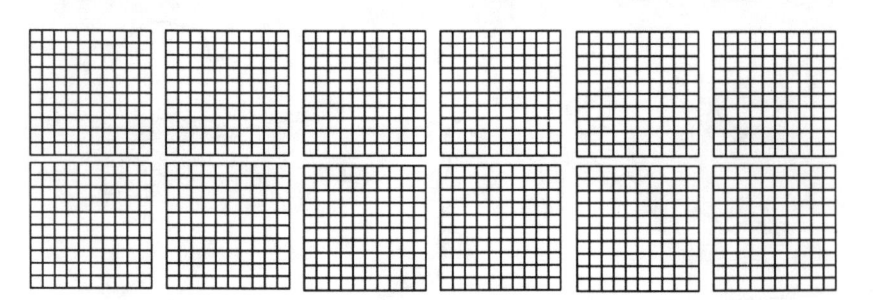

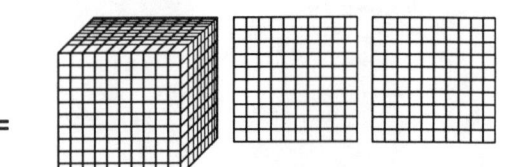

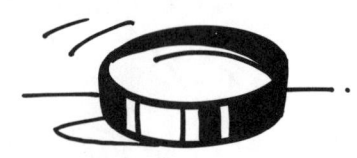

12 hundreds = 1 thousand 2 hundreds

1. Add ones. Ask: Do I need to regroup?

```
  5 2 6
+ 7 3 2
      8
```

2. Add tens. Ask: Do I need to regroup?

```
  5 2 6
+ 7 3 2
    5 8
```

3. Add hundreds. Ask: Do I need to regroup?

```
  5 2 6
+ 7 3 2
1 2 5 8
```

12 hundreds = 1 thousand 2 hundreds

Wordsearch!
Find: Crossword puzzle addition is a blast!

```
M Q N Y X U P E S A
W C R O S S W O R D
B V P C V Y F L T D
Z P R U W G U M O I
L H O E Z B L A S T
X I A H J Z I N C I
Q D J C F S L R K O
K Z I S G T B E D N
```

Add. Regroup when needed.

```
  7 2 4        3 4 2        7 2 9
+ 6 4 3      + 9 3 6      + 6 4 3


  5 0 8        5 8 3        8 4 6
+ 8 1 8      + 4 2 5      + 2 3 9
```

Math IF5104

Puzzling Problems

Addition — Regrouping Hundreds

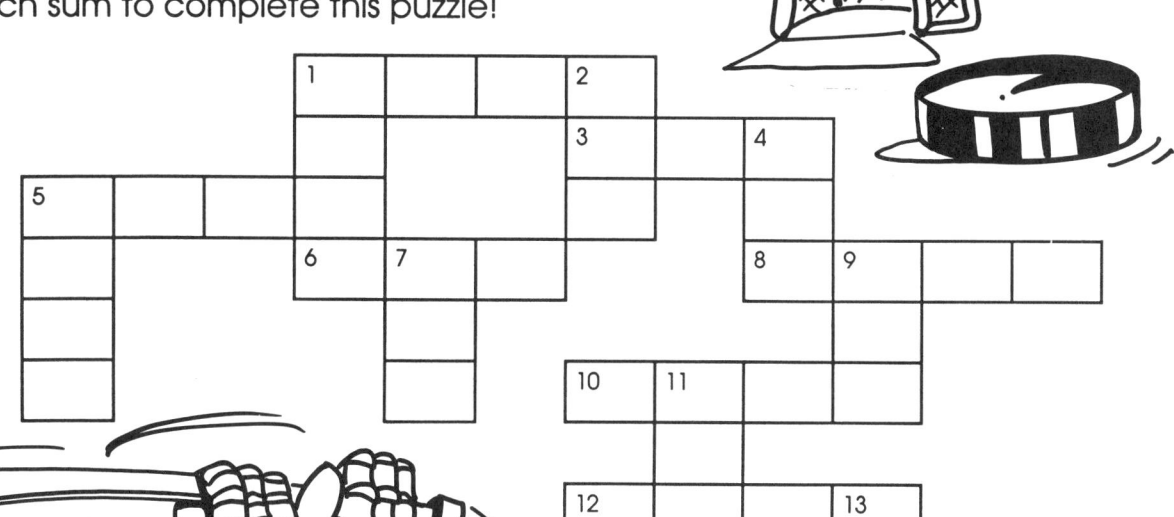

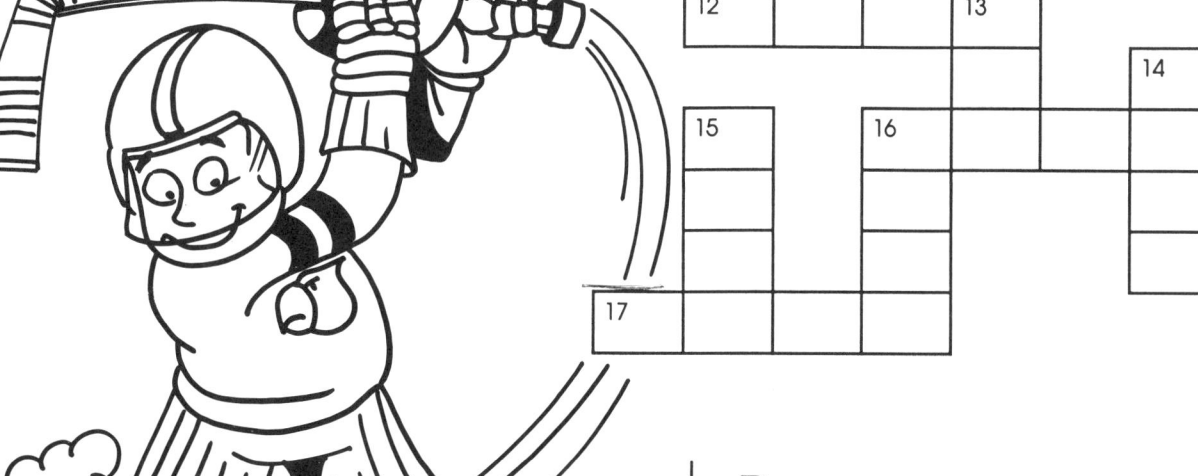

Find each sum to complete this puzzle!

Across

1. 548
   +629

3. 381
   +456

5. 265
   +845

6. 387
   +493

8. 919
   +819

10. 642
   +793

12. 912
   +693

16. 824
   +423

17. 895
   +909

Down

1. 527
   +681

2. 538
   +246

4. 536
   +195

5. 963
   +282

7. 248
   +623

9. 368
   +347

11. 189
   +267

13. 267
   +285

14. 824
   +890

15. 993
   +795

16. 946
   +238

Math IF5104 — 13 — ©MCMXCIV Instructional Fair, Inc.

Four-Digit Addition With Regrouping

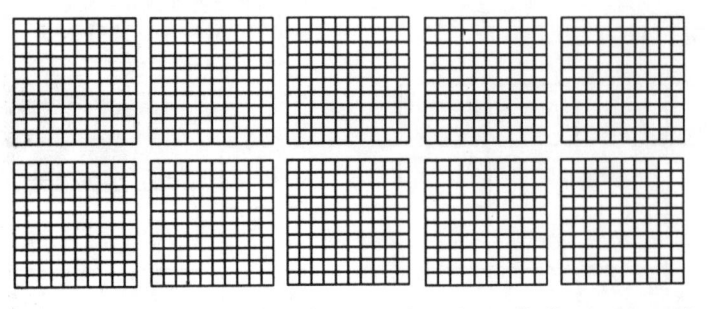

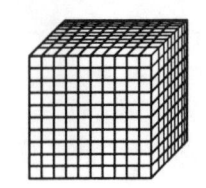

10 hundreds = 1 thousand

1. Add ones. Ask: Do I need to regroup?

$$3\,4\,^{1}2\,8$$
$$+2\,7\,1\,4$$
$$2$$

2. Add tens. Ask: Do I need to regroup?

$$3\,4\,^{1}2\,8$$
$$+2\,7\,1\,4$$
$$4\,2$$

3. Add hundreds. Ask: Do I need to regroup?

$$^{1}3\,4\,^{1}2\,8$$
$$+2\,7\,1\,4$$
$$1\,4\,2$$

4. Add thousands. Ask: Do I need to regroup?

$$^{1}3\,4\,^{1}2\,8$$
$$+2\,7\,1\,4$$
$$6\,1\,4\,2$$

Did You Know?

* 1,000 pennies = $10.00!

* 1,000 years is called a millennium!

* 1,000 x 1,000 = 1,000,000 (one million)!

* The Earth rotates on its axis at (about) 1,000 miles per hour!

Add. Regroup when needed.

```
  3 4 1 5        5 3 4 0        2 4 2 8
 +2 9 5 3       +1 8 2 8       +3 1 9 7

        6 4 8 2        9 4 2 6        3 4 5 6
       +1 7 0 5       +  3 8 2       +6 6 1 9
```

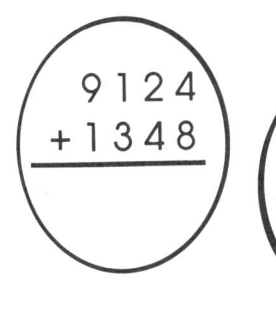

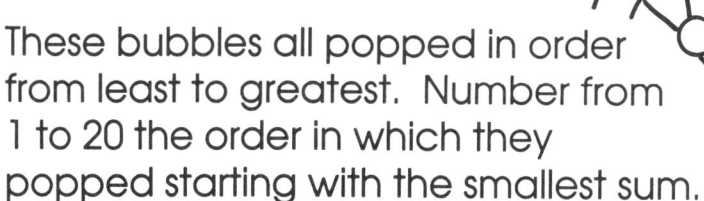

Bubble Math

Four-Digit Addition With Regrouping

Add the problems inside these bubbles.

- 5642 + 1819
- 4629 + 1258
- 2647 + 3281
- 3426 + 2841
- 3690 + 2434
- 4625 + 1817
- 6843 + 2391
- 6241 + 2363
- 5942 + 1829
- 5642 + 2919
- 2648 + 1923
- 4826 + 2098
- 2641 + 6259
- 8465 + 1386
- 7205 + 1839
- 2643 + 7427
- 5246 + 3187
- 4265 + 3827
- 9124 + 1348
- 3142 + 2639

These bubbles all popped in order from least to greatest. Number from 1 to 20 the order in which they popped starting with the smallest sum.

Four-Digit Addition With Regrouping

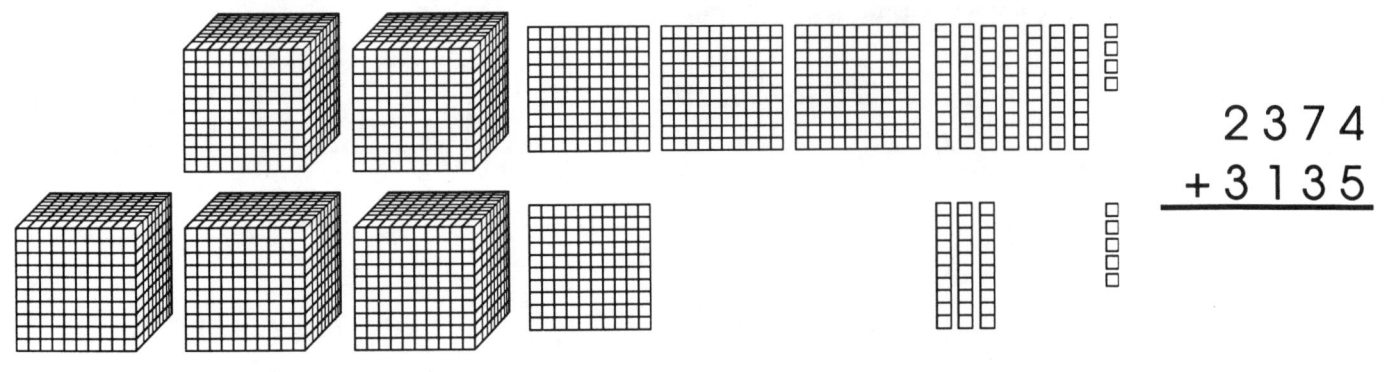

thousands   hundreds   tens   ones

```
  2 3 7 4
+ 3 1 3 5
```

1. Add ones. Ask: Do I need to regroup?

```
  2 3 7 4
+ 3 1 3 5
────────
        9
```

2. Add tens. Ask: Do I need to regroup?

```
  2¹3 7 4
+ 3 1 3 5
────────
      0 9
```

3. Add hundreds. Ask: Do I need to regroup?

```
  2¹3 7 4
+ 3 1 3 5
────────
    5 0 9
```

4. Add thousands. Ask: Do I need to regroup?

```
  2¹3 7 4
+ 3 1 3 5
────────
  5 5 0 9
```

Add. Regroup when needed.

```
  6208          5416              7526
+ 1913        + 5298            + 2484

         2352           2671            3614
       + 1292         + 3619          + 2902
```

Shape Up Your Addition!

Four-Digit Addition With Regrouping

Add. Regroup when needed. In each row, circle the greatest sum, draw a box around the least sum, and draw a triangle around the sum in between. Fill in the chart at the bottom of the page.

	Column A	**Column B**	**Column C**
Row 1	3462 +4183	5614 +1892	5265 +5342
Row 2	8241 +1792	6424 +2849	6329 +1839
Row 3	2435 +4918	7421 +2394	3614 +2434
Row 4	8216 +1398	3641 +4197	2684 +5297
Row 5	3814 +4209	7428 +1397	5432 +4819
Row 6	7614 +2984	7346 +2175	9246 +1084

Match each column pattern starting with row 6.

Letter: **Repeat each pattern:**

___   △ O △ □ □ O   _____

___   □ △ □ O △ □   _____

___   O □ O △ O △   _____

Addition of Money

In two months, Andy earned these amounts:

How much did he earn altogether?

$41.³¹31
+ 8.49
———————
$49.80

> When adding money, always line up the decimal points.
>
> $6 . ¹42
> . 08
> + 4 . 20
> ————————
> $10 ↓ 70
>
> Then, when you find the total, add a decimal point (.) and a dollar sign ($) to the answer (the sum).

Here's what was in Eva's piggy bank!

$ .05   one nickel
    3.00   three dollars
+   .75   three quarters
————————

How much does she have?

Add. Regroup when needed.

$4.06 $3.64 $3.94
+ .84   + 2.91   + 2.23

$21.32 $86.09 $4.87
+ 43.98   + 28.47   + 7.96

Math IF5104 — 18 — ©MCMXCIV Instructional Fair, Inc.

Monetary Message

Addition of Money

What's the smartest thing to do with your money? To find out, use the key at the bottom of the page to match the letters with the sums in the blanks provided.

___ ___ ___ ___   ___ ___ ___
$42.71 $33.94 $50.42 $100.73 $45.70 $2.39 $1.55

___ ___ ___   ___ ___   ___ ___ ___ ___
$33.94 $26.13 $88.02 $45.70 $2.39 $51.12 $45.70 $11.01 $11.01

___ ___ ___   ___ ___ ___
$33.94 $88.02 $88.02 $55.76 $42.79 $6.84

V = $42.13 + 8.29

A = $4.56 + 29.38

N = $4.65 + 21.48

, = $.09 + 1.25 + .21

P = $9.31 + 33.48

L = $6.73 + 4.28

E = $81.49 + 19.24

T = $.42 + 1.94 + .03

U = $50.84 + 4.92

I = $7.49 + 38.21

S = $23.46 + 19.25

D = $3.04 + 84.98

W = $1.89 + 49.23

! = $4.35 + 2.49

Math IF5104 19 ©MCMXCIV Instructional Fair, Inc.

Addition of Money

Add money the same way you add regular addition problems. When you finish, be sure to add the decimal point (.) and the dollar sign ($).

Samuel bought
the guitar: $48.99
and skateboard: + 31.47

What is his total?

Esther bought
the rollerblades: $24.69
and guitar: + 48.99

What is her total?

Add. Regroup when needed. Place the decimal point (.) and dollar sign ($) in the sum.

$49.03
+ 8.94

$61.82
+ 13.97

$24.38
+ 12.90

$2.98
+ 8.31

$80.49
+ 9.80

$ 8.32
+ 10.86

Hats, Hats, Hats

Subtraction — Regrouping Ones

Calculate the difference in each hat below.

736 − 629

466 − 327

837 − 529

742 − 428

784 − 565

673 − 458

648 − 426

982 − 665

947 − 729

543 − 426

928 − 619

847 − 628

427 − 318

524 − 318

245 − 126

852 − 328

545 − 221

Subtraction — Regrouping Ones

Problem: 6 4 3
         −4 2 6

The One's Column

1. <u>The First Question</u>: Can I take 6 from 3? No.

    6 4 3
    −4 2 6

2. Borrow one ten and regroup.

    6 ³4̸ ¹3
    −4 2 6

    1 ten = 10 ones

3. Subtract.

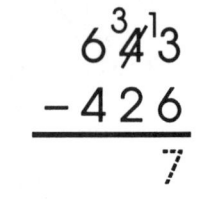

    6 ³4̸ ¹3
    −4 2 6
    ─────
          7

The Ten's Column

4. <u>The Second Question</u>: Can I take 2 from 3? Yes. Subtract.

    6 ³4̸ ¹3
    −4 2 6
    ─────
       1 7

The Hundred's Column

5. <u>The Third Question</u>: Can I take 4 from 6? Yes. Subtract.

    6 ³4̸ ¹3
    −4 2 6
    ─────
    2 1 7

Subtract. Regroup when needed.

    9 2 5   7 6 8   8 3 6
    −4 1 6   −5 3 9   −5 1 7

    5 4 6   9 7 4   4 7 3
    −3 2 8   −3 5 2   −2 4 6

Surprise! Surprise!

Subtraction — Regrouping Ones

Connect the dots to create two surprises! Counting forward, start with the subtraction problem whose difference is 100 and end with the problem whose difference is 109. Then, begin again with 110 and connect the consecutive dots to 120. Color in the pictures when you are finished.

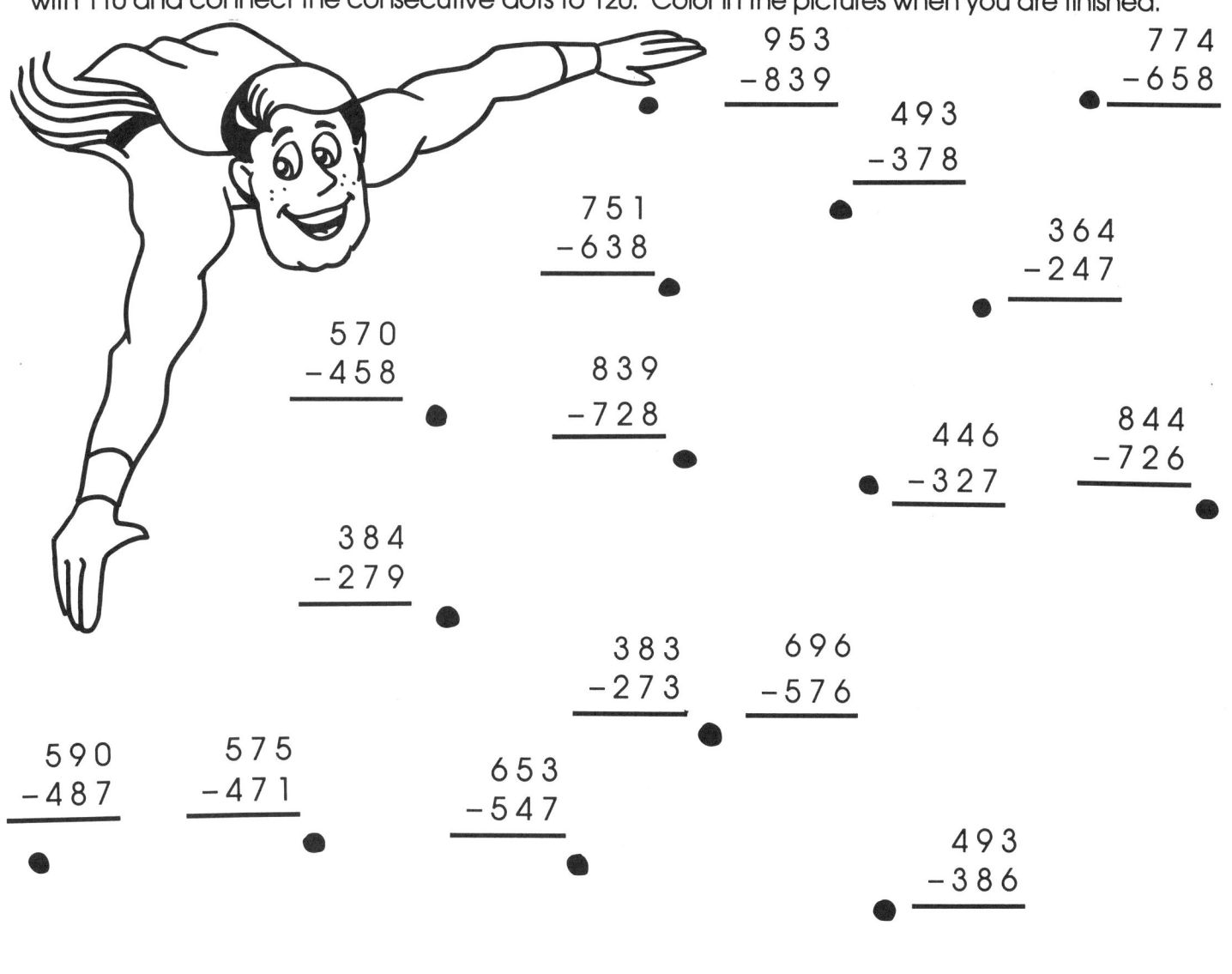

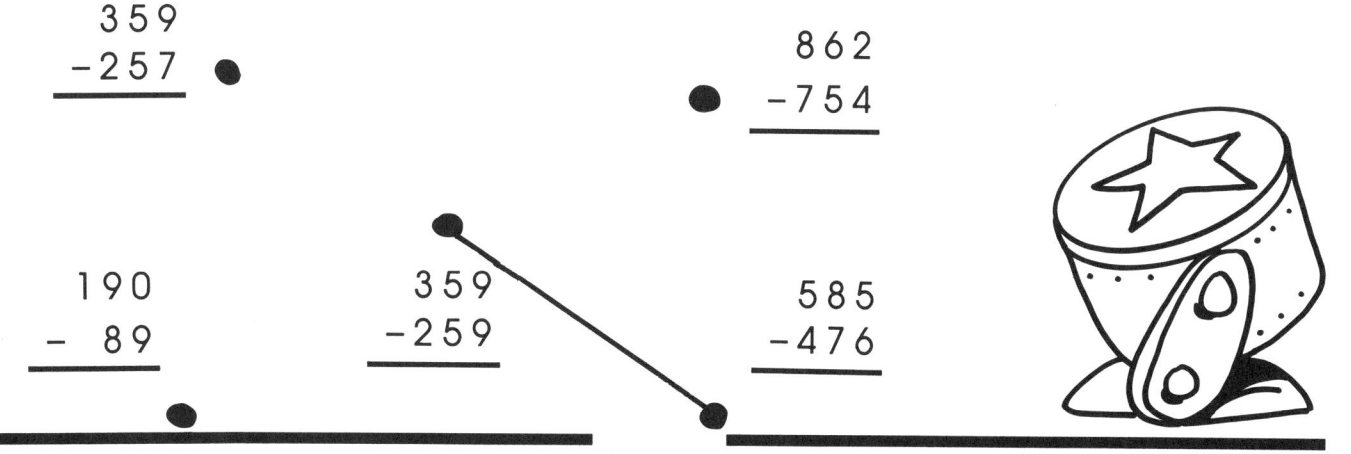

```
  953          774
 -839         -658
 ----         ----
        493
       -378
       ----
  751          364
 -638         -247
 ----         ----
570     839
-458   -728
----   ----
              446      844
             -327     -726
             ----     ----
384
-279
----
       383    696
      -273   -576
      ----   ----
590    575
-487   -471    653
----   ----   -547
              ----
                      493
                     -386
                     ----
359
-257
              862
             -754
             ----
190    359            585
- 89   -259          -476
----   ----          ----
```

Math IF5104   ©MCMXCIV Instructional Fair, Inc.

Subtraction — Regrouping Tens

There were 348 kids on bikes and 163 kids on rollerblades. How many more were getting around on bikes?

1. Subtract ones. Ask: Do I need to regroup?

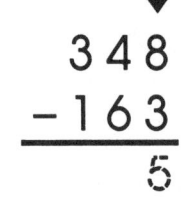

    ```
      348
    - 163
    ─────
        5
    ```

2. Subtract tens. Ask: Do I need to regroup?

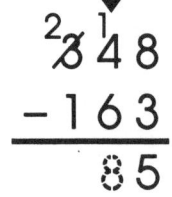

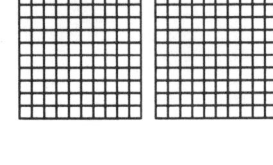

    ```
     ²3¹48
    - 163
    ─────
       85
    ```

    1 hundred = 10 tens

3. Subtract hundreds.

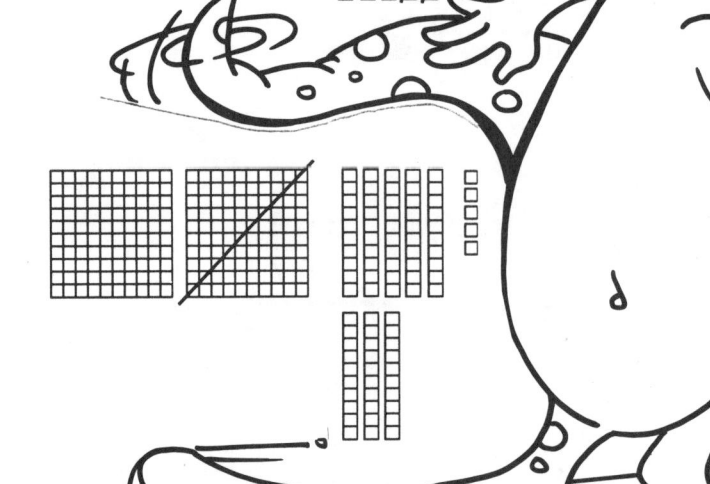

    ```
     ²3¹48
    - 163
    ─────
      185
    ```

Subtract. Regroup when needed.

```
  857        346        468
 -462       -172       -294
 ────       ────       ────

             928                  729
            -495                 -568
```
```
             564
            -381
```

Dino-Might

Subtraction — Regrouping Tens

Whenever you're using "kid transportation," what is the best thing to do? To find out, use the key at the bottom of the page to match the letters with the differences in the blanks provided.

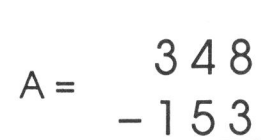

___ ___ ___ ___ ___ ___
195 92   265 195 185 45

___ ___ ___ ___   ___
265 171 195 183   195

___ ___ ___ ___ ___ ___ ___
181 171 92   93   171 191 74

A = 348 − 153

L = 765 − 673

S = 427 − 382

M = 568 − 475

T = 637 − 446

H = 878 − 697

Y = 548 − 363

W = 748 − 483

E = 824 − 653

R = 439 − 256

! = 447 − 373

Subtraction — Regrouping Tens

The One's Column

1. <u>The First Question</u>: Can I take 2 from 5? Yes. Subtract.

```
  8 3 5
 -4 7 2
      3
```

The Ten's Column

2. <u>The Second Question</u>: Can I take 7 from 3? No.

```
  8 3 5
 -4 7 2
      3
```

3. Borrow one hundred and regroup.

```
  ⁷8̷ ¹3 5
 -4 7 2
        3
```
1 hundred = 10 tens

4. Subtract.

```
  ⁷8̷ ¹3 5
 -4 7 2
     6 3
```

The Hundred's Column

5. <u>The Third Question</u>: Can I take 4 from 7? Yes. Subtract.

```
  ⁷8̷ ¹3 5
 -4 7 2
  3 6 3
```

Subtract. Regroup when needed.

```
  7 3 8        9 3 6         8 4 7
 -4 6 2       -4 8 5        -6 3 5


  9 4 6        6 2 5         7 6 3
 -3 5 4       -4 6 3        -5 8 1
```

Find the Hidden Instrument!

Subtraction — Regrouping Tens

Solve each problem. Color each shape according to the key below.

482

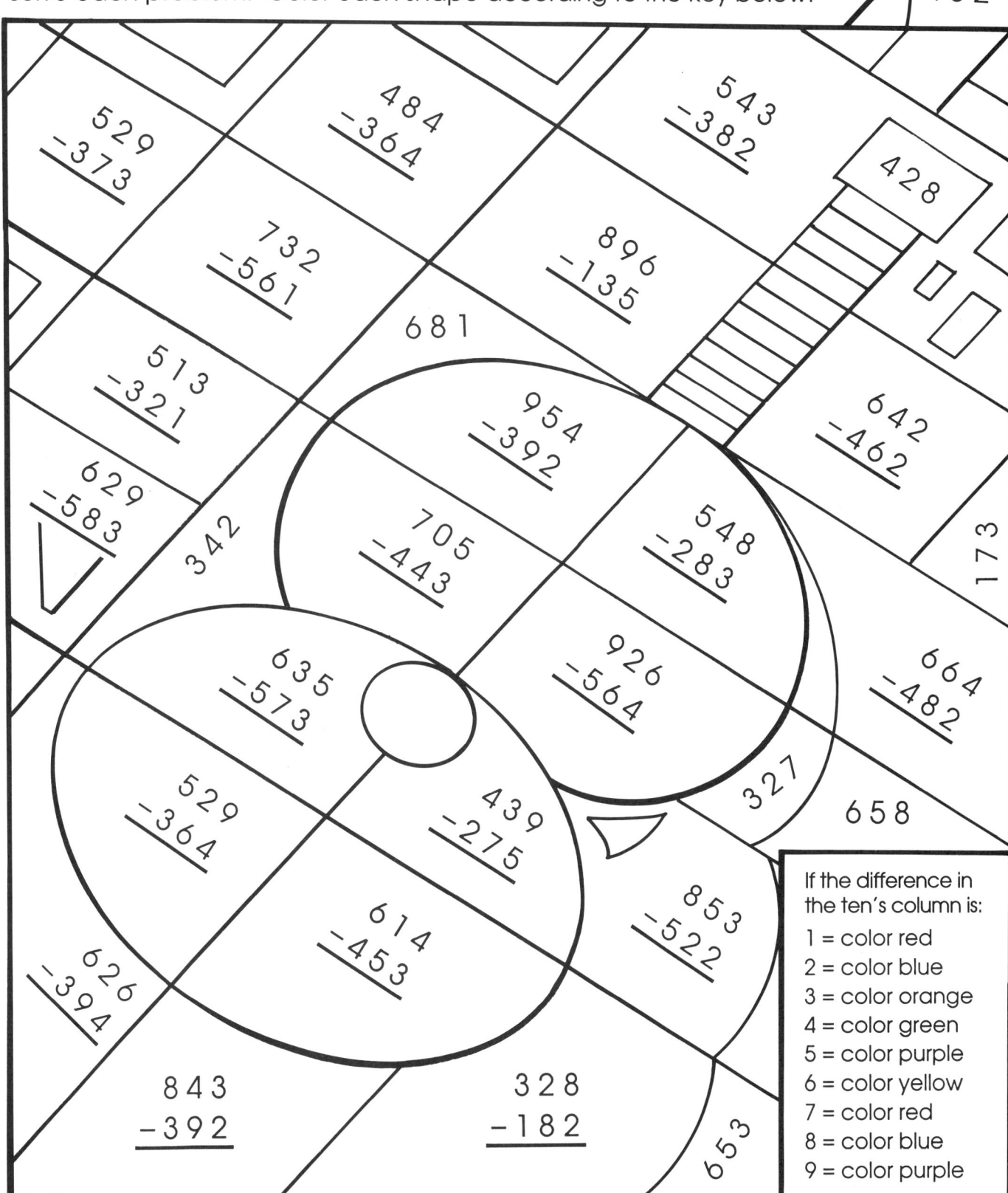

529
−373

484
−364

543
−382

428

732
−561

896
−135

513
−321

642
−462

629
−583

954
−392

342

705
−443

548
−283

681

635
−573

926
−564

173

529
−364

439
−275

664
−482

614
−453

327

626
−394

853
−522

658

843
−392

328
−182

653

If the difference in the ten's column is:

1 = color red
2 = color blue
3 = color orange
4 = color green
5 = color purple
6 = color yellow
7 = color red
8 = color blue
9 = color purple

Math IF5104

29

©MCMXCIV Instructional Fair, Inc.

Subtraction — Regrouping Tens and Ones

The subtraction sailors have sailed a total of 324 miles in the past two days. Yesterday, they zoomed a total of 147 miles through the blue ocean. How many miles did they sail today?

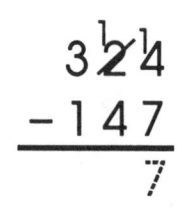

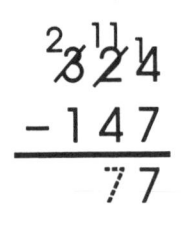

1. Subtract ones. Ask: Do I need to regroup?

$$\begin{array}{r} 3\overset{1}{2}\overset{}{4} \\ -1\,4\,7 \\ \hline 7 \end{array}$$

2. Subtract tens. Ask: Do I need to regroup?

$$\begin{array}{r} \overset{2}{\cancel{3}}\overset{11}{\cancel{2}}\overset{}{4} \\ -1\,4\,7 \\ \hline 7\,7 \end{array}$$

3. Subtract hundreds.

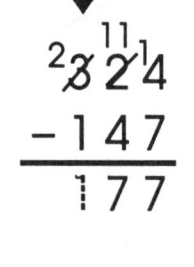

$$\begin{array}{r} \overset{2}{\cancel{3}}\overset{11}{\cancel{2}}\overset{}{4} \\ -1\,4\,7 \\ \hline 1\,7\,7 \end{array}$$

$$\begin{array}{r} 3\,2\,4 \text{ total}\\ -1\,4\,7 \text{ first day}\\ \hline 1\,7\,7 \text{ today} \end{array}$$

Subtract. Regroup when needed.

$$\begin{array}{r} 643 \\ -258 \\ \hline \end{array} \qquad \begin{array}{r} 429 \\ -284 \\ \hline \end{array} \qquad \begin{array}{r} 967 \\ -488 \\ \hline \end{array} \qquad \begin{array}{r} 721 \\ -564 \\ \hline \end{array} \qquad \begin{array}{r} 523 \\ -457 \\ \hline \end{array} \qquad \begin{array}{r} 329 \\ -186 \\ \hline \end{array}$$

Math IF5104 ©MCMXCIV Instructional Fair, Inc.

Sailing Through Subtraction

Subtraction — Regrouping Tens and Ones

Start at the bottom and work your way up the sails.

```
 542      638           836      737
-383     -453          -478     -448
```

```
 243      567           984      468
-154     -384          -643     -399
```

```
 524      674           374      246
-342     -495          -185     -158
```

```
 852      736           642      435
-464     -557          -557     -286
```

Subtraction — Regrouping Tens and Ones

The One's Column

1. <u>The First Question</u>: Can I take 6 from 4? No.

   ```
     5 3 4
   - 3 4 6
   ```

2. Borrow one ten and regroup. Subtract.

   ```
     5 ²3̸ ¹4̸
   - 3 4 6
         8
   ```
   1 ten = 10 ones

The Ten's Column

3. <u>The Second Question</u>: Can I take 4 from 2? No.

   ```
     5 ²3̸ ¹4̸
   - 3 4 6
         8
   ```

4. Borrow one hundred and regroup. Subtract.

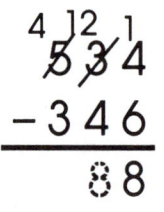

   ```
     ⁴5̸ ¹²3̸ ¹4̸
   - 3 4 6
       8 8
   ```
   1 hundred = 10 tens

The Hundred's Column

5. <u>The Third Question</u>: Can I take 3 from 4? Yes. Subtract.

   ```
     ⁴5̸ ¹²3̸ ¹4̸
   - 3 4 6
     1 8 8
   ```

Subtract. Regroup when needed.

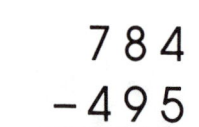

```
  6 2 3        3 4 8        4 6 5
- 4 3 5      - 2 5 4      - 2 8 6


        8 4 6        9 5 7        7 8 4
      - 5 8 7      - 5 8 8      - 4 9 5
```

Secret Salutation

Subtraction — Regrouping Tens and Ones

What is Monica saying to everyone out in Subtractionland? To find out, use the key at the bottom of the page to match the letters with the differences in the blanks provided.

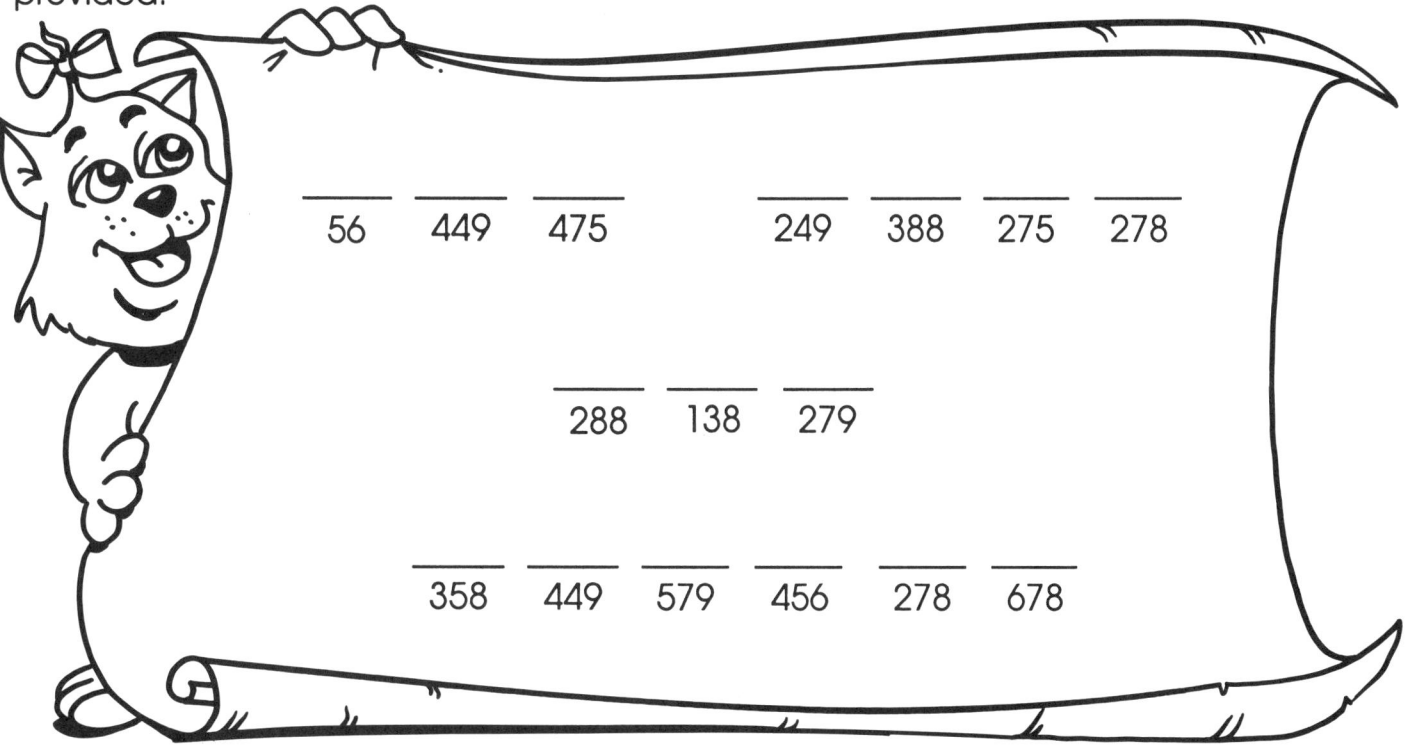

___ ___ ___   ___ ___ ___ ___
56   449 475   249 388 275 278

___ ___ ___
288 138 279

___ ___ ___ ___ ___ ___
358 449 579 456 278 678

Key:

O = 524 − 136

D = 518 − 239

H = 324 − 268

L = 624 − 168

I = 846 − 397

G = 642 − 284

B = 418 − 169

! = 916 − 238

S = 427 − 149

R = 825 − 246

, = 821 − 346

N = 234 − 96

Y = 521 − 246

A = 467 − 179

Subtraction With Zeros

On Saturday, 400 students visited Zoomland. 238 rode the "zoom car." How many didn't have time?

1. Borrow one group of one hundred. Cross out and make one less.

   ³4̸00
   −238

2. Convert to 10 tens.

   ³4̸¹00
   −238

   1 hundred = 10 tens

3. Borrow one group of tens, regroup in the one's column.

   ³4̸⁹1̸0̸0
   −238

   1 ten = 10 ones

4. Subtract. Begin at one's column.

   ³4̸⁹1̸0̸0
   −238
   162

Subtract. Regroup when needed.

   300   600   800
   −146   −338   −743

              208   502   200
              −142   −193   −136

Round and Round She Goes...

Subtraction With Zeros

Take a ride around this ferris wheel.

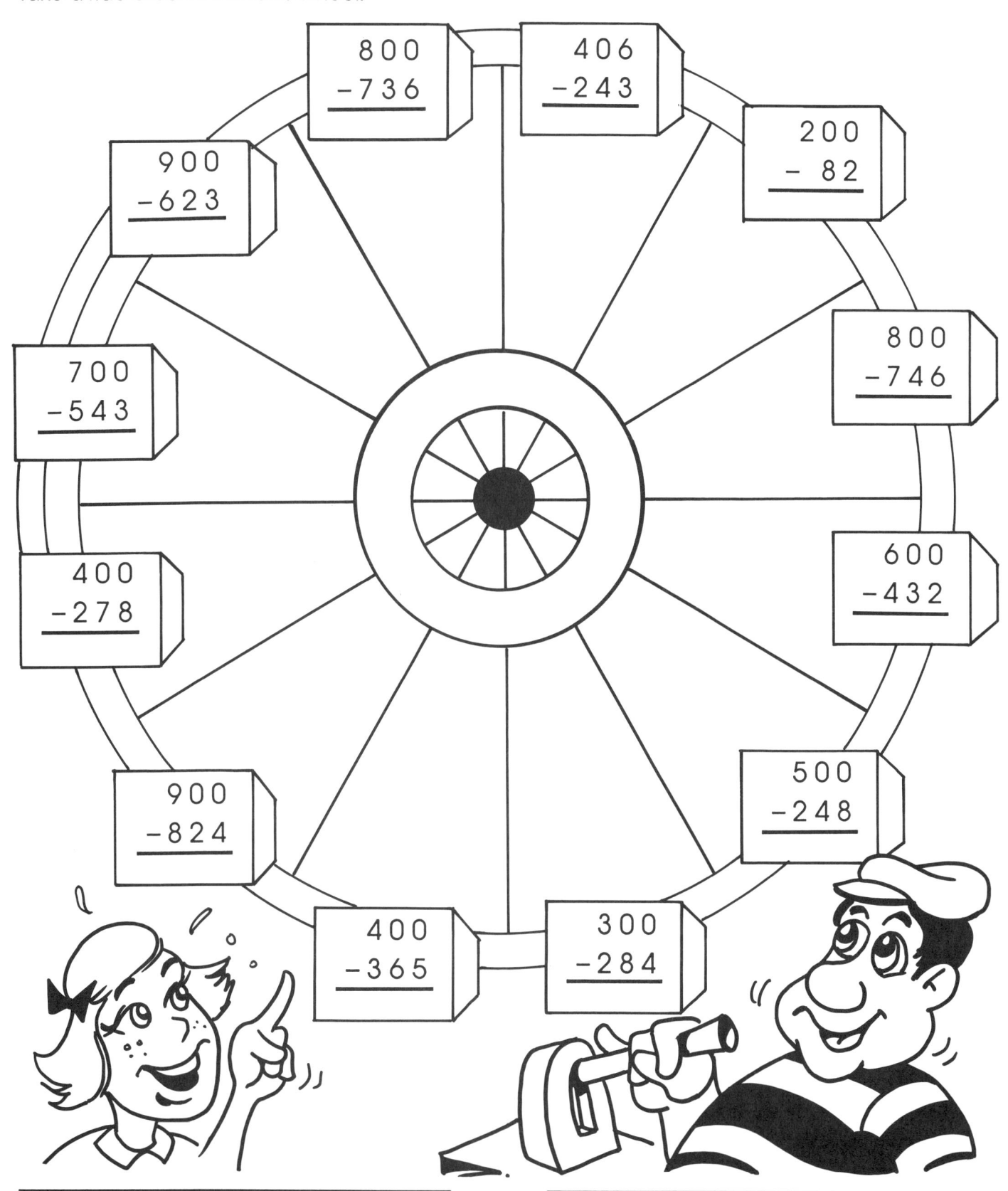

- 800 − 736
- 406 − 243
- 200 − 82
- 900 − 623
- 800 − 746
- 700 − 543
- 600 − 432
- 400 − 278
- 500 − 248
- 900 − 824
- 400 − 365
- 300 − 284

Subtraction With Zeros

500 swimmers went to the pool to enjoy the refreshment of swimming. 247 used the diving board. How many swimmers didn't?

1. Ask: Do I need to regroup?

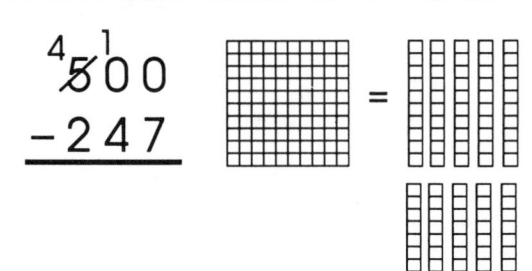

$$\begin{array}{r} \overset{4}{\cancel{5}}\overset{1}{0}0 \\ -247 \\ \hline \end{array}$$

1 hundred = 10 tens

2. Regroup again.

$$\begin{array}{r} \overset{4}{\cancel{5}}\overset{1}{\cancel{0}}\overset{9}{0} \\ -247 \\ \hline \end{array}$$

1 ten = 10 ones

3. Now, you're ready to subtract. Begin at the one's column.

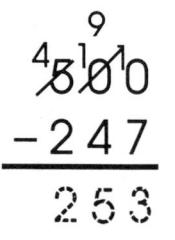

$$\begin{array}{r} \overset{4}{\cancel{5}}\overset{1}{\cancel{0}}\overset{9}{0} \\ -247 \\ \hline 253 \end{array}$$

253 swimmers chose not to use the board!

Subtract. Regroup when needed.

$$\begin{array}{r} 900 \\ -285 \\ \hline \end{array} \qquad \begin{array}{r} 600 \\ -457 \\ \hline \end{array} \qquad \begin{array}{r} 803 \\ -646 \\ \hline \end{array} \qquad \begin{array}{r} 200 \\ -84 \\ \hline \end{array} \qquad \begin{array}{r} 500 \\ -249 \\ \hline \end{array} \qquad \begin{array}{r} 407 \\ -284 \\ \hline \end{array}$$

Math IF5104

Dive Into Subtraction!

Subtraction With Zeros

Complete the puzzle by solving the problems below.

Across

1. 600
   −247

4. 800
   −145

6. 800
   −527

7. 200
   −172

8. 807
   −142

9. 904
   −285

11. 600
   −427

12. 903
   −624

13. 900
   −264

15. 800
   −386

17. 800
   −527

Down

2. 700
   −184

3. 900
   −448

5. 900
   −764

7. 500
   −243

10. 400
   −248

11. 500
   −304

14. 800
   −138

15. 708
   −269

16. 900
   −468

Math IF5104

37

©MCMXCIV Instructional Fair, Inc.

Four-Digit Subtraction With Regrouping

The Windy Breeze Kite Co. made 3,426 kites to sell. After one week, they had 1,619 remaining. How many did they sell the first week?

1. Subtract ones. Ask: Do I need to regroup?

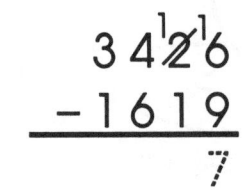

   3 4 2̷¹ 6̸¹
   - 1 6 1 9
   ———————
            7

   1 ten = 10 ones

2. Subtract tens. Ask: Do I need to regroup?

   3 4 2̷¹ 6̸¹
   - 1 6 1 9
   ———————
         0 7

3. Subtract hundreds. Ask: Do I need to regroup?

   ²3̷ 4̷¹ 2̷¹ 6̸¹
   - 1 6 1 9
   ———————
       8 0 7

   1 thousand = 10 hundreds

4. Subtract thousands.

   ²3̷ 4̷¹ 2̷¹ 6̸¹
   - 1 6 1 9
   ———————
     1 8 0 7

Subtract. Regroup when needed.

   6 4 8 5
   - 2 3 5 4
   ————————

   7 6 4 8
   - 5 7 2 7
   ————————

   3 8 4 7
   - 2 5 9 9
   ————————

   8 1 0 4
   - 6 0 4 3
   ————————

   9 4 6 3
   - 4 8 2 5
   ————————

   5 8 4 7
   - 2 4 9 8
   ————————

Kite Craze!

Four-Digit Subtraction With Regrouping

Subtract. How will you get way up there to solve the problems?

8794
−6428

9643
−8825

8825
−7436

5648
−3929

7005
−6223

8416
−3509

4162
−2840

6514
−3282

5436
−2924

9246
−8518

4862
−3946

9486
−6294

9085
−6241

8462
−6391

7643
−6521

6430
−4252

Four-Digit Subtraction With Regrouping

The One's Column

1. <u>The First Question</u>: Can I take 5 from 4? No.

```
  8294
- 2635
```

2. Borrow one ten and regroup. Subtract.

```
     8 1
  8 2 9 4
- 2 6 3 5
        9
```

1 ten = 10 ones

The Ten's Column

3. <u>The Second Question</u>: Can I take 3 from 8? Yes. Subtract.

```
     8 1
  8 2 9 4
- 2 6 3 5
      5 9
```

The Hundred's Column

4. <u>The Third Question</u>: Can I take 6 from 2? No.

```
     8 1
  8 2 9 4
- 2 6 3 5
      5 9
```

5. Borrow one thousand and regroup. Subtract.

```
  7 18 1
  8 2 9 4
- 2 6 3 5
    6 5 9
```

1 thousand = 10 hundreds

The Thousand's Column

6. <u>The Third Question</u>: Can I take 2 from 7? Yes. Subtract.

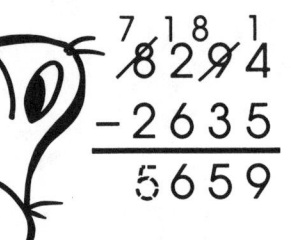

```
  7 18 1
  8 2 9 4
- 2 6 3 5
  5 6 5 9
```

Subtract. Regroup when needed.

```
  5642        8409         7562
- 1821       -1182        -1681

              8923         4628
             -1364        -1714        4238
                                      -1449
```

Subtraction on Stage!

Four-Digit Subtraction With Regrouping

These subtraction problems are heading west. Solve 'em. It'll be a bouncy ride. Just hold on!

```
 5648        2148        7641        7648
-2425       - 825       -5246       -3289
-----       -----       -----       -----

 5408        8209        8419        6249
-1291       -4182       -2182       -1526
-----       -----       -----       -----

 6428        4287        7645        2016
-4159       -2492       -2826       -1021
-----       -----       -----       -----

                                     7689
                                    -2845
                                    -----

 8247        9047        5231
-6459       -6152       -1642
-----       -----       -----
```

Math IF5104

41

©MCMXCIV Instructional Fair, Inc.

Subtraction of Money

Jamaica earned $42.43 selling vegetables from her garden. She spent $11.28 on seeds and gardening tools to replant. How much money did she have left?

Problem: $42.43
         − 11.28

1. When subtracting, make sure the decimal points line up.

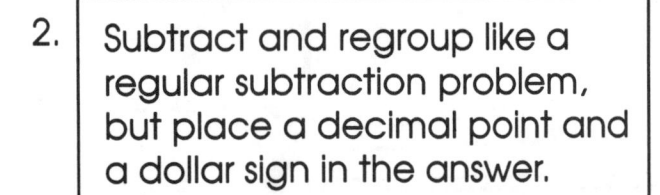

   $42.43
   − 11.28

2. Subtract and regroup like a regular subtraction problem, but place a decimal point and a dollar sign in the answer.

   $42.⁳ⁱ43
   − 11.28
   $31.15

Subtract. Regroup when needed.

$8.46 $5.06 $7.43
− 5.92   − 3.42   − 3.86

        $32.40 $10.46 $24.36
        − 18.24   − 8.23   − 12.47

Math IF5104   42   ©MCMXCIV Instructional Fair, Inc.

Spending Spree

Subtraction of Money

Use the clues to figure out what each child bought. Then, subtract to find out how much change each had left.

Clue:

1. Katelyn started with: $23.45 — She likes to keep warm!

2. David began with: $40.25 — He loves to see things zoom into the sky!

3. Mark started with: $50.37 — He likes to travel places with his hands free and a breeze in his face!

4. Eva started with: $14.84 — She loves to practice her jumping and exercise at the same time!

5. Earl arrived with: $26.42 — He loves to learn about interesting things!

6. Bill brought: $61.49 — He wants to see the heavens for himself!

7. Michelle brought: $40.29 — Fuzzy companions make such great friends!

8. Cheryl started with: $16.80 — She loves to hear music that is soft and beautiful!

9. Heather arrived with: $20.48 — She loves to put it down on paper for everyone to see!

$9.31 $12.49 $52.28 $15.29 $2.43 $13.45 $21.52 $32.51 $3.95 $47.29

Math IF5104   43   ©MCMXCIV Instructional Fair, Inc.

ANSWER KEY
Addition and Subtraction
Grade 3

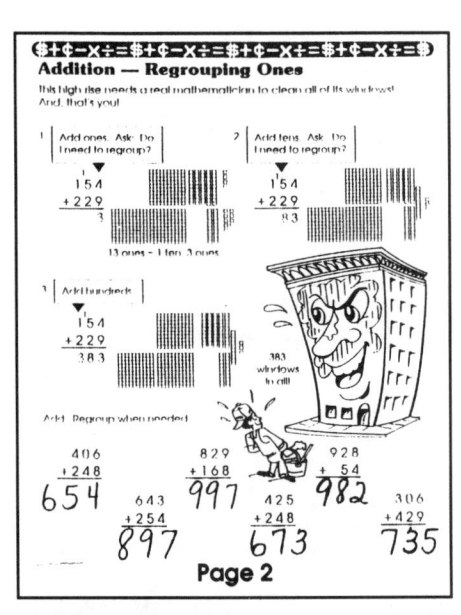

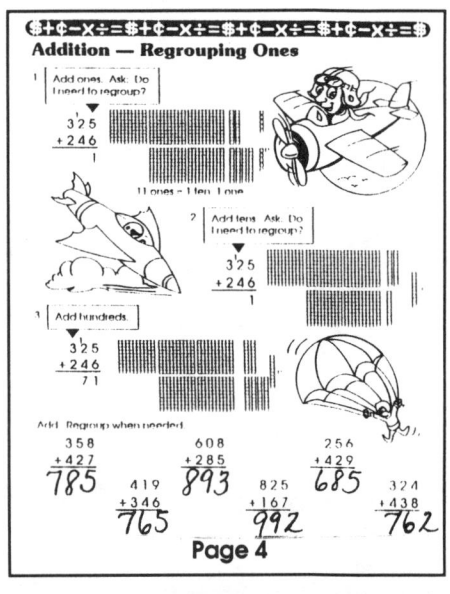

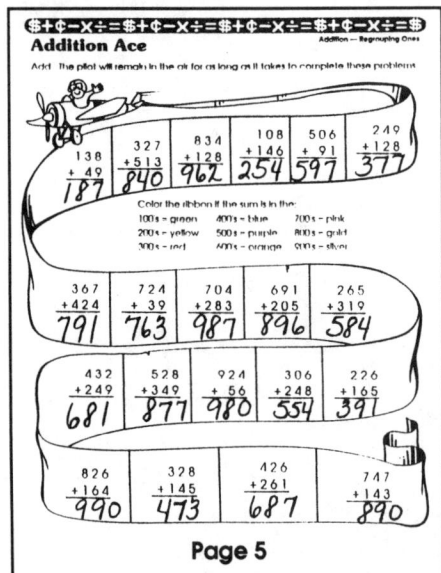

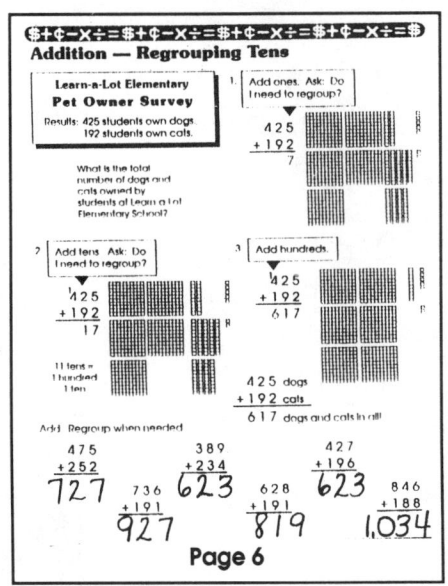

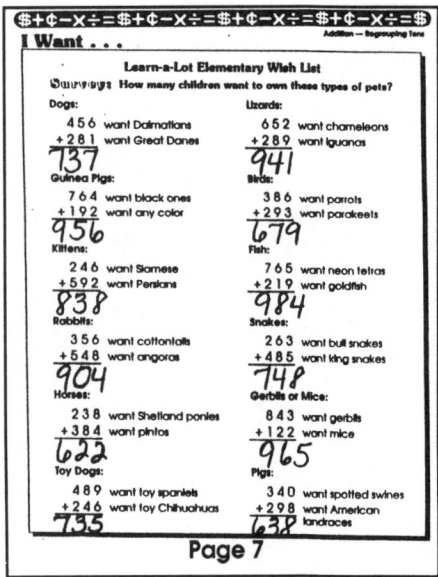

44

Math IF5104 ©MCMXCIV Instructional Fair, Inc.

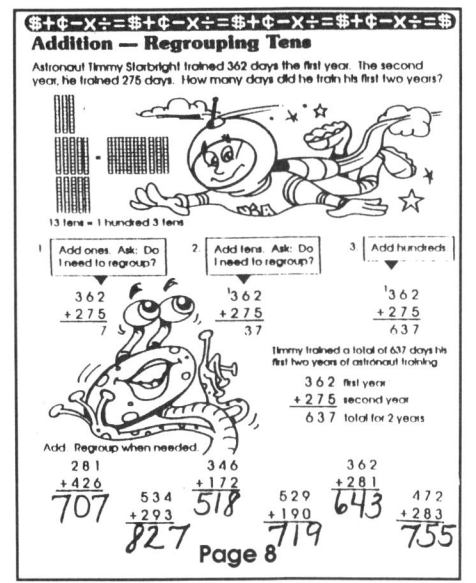

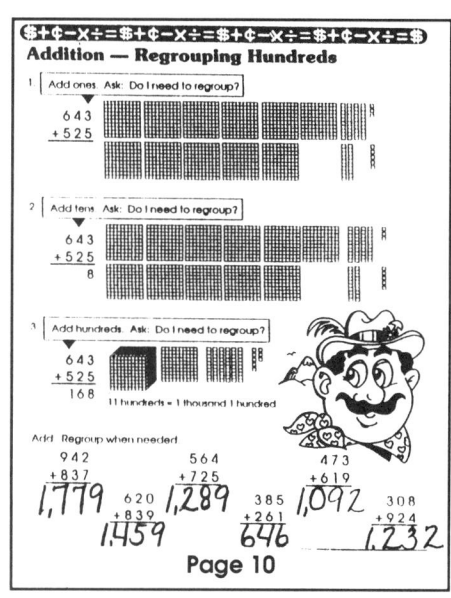

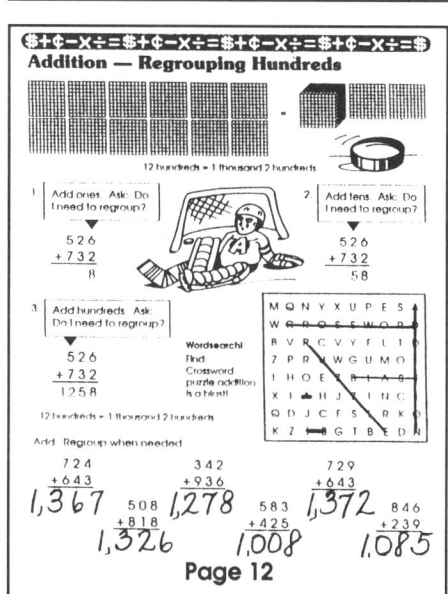

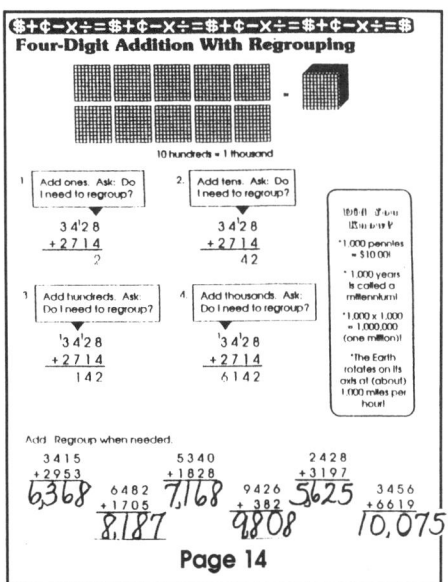

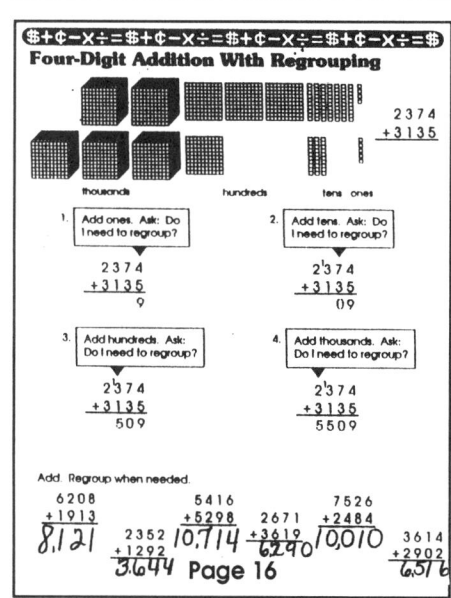

Page 8 — Addition — Regrouping Tens

Astronaut Timmy Starbright trained 362 days the first year. The second year, he trained 275 days. How many days did he train his first two years?

Timmy trained a total of 637 days his first two years of astronaut training.

362 first year
+275 second year
637 total for 2 years

Add. Regroup when needed.

281 + 426 = 707
346 + 172 = 518
534 + 293 = 827
529 + 190 = 719
362 + 281 = 643
472 + 283 = 755

Page 9 — Space Shuttle Addition

371 + ... = 810
264 + 483 = 747
629 + 184 = 813
146 + 587 = 733
362 + ... = 827
438 + 290 = 728
347 + 328 = 675
327 + ... = 919
528 + 391 = 919
346 + ... = 631
465 + ... = 658
566 + ... = 629
409 + ... = 701
423 + ... = 849
566 + 283 = 849
625 + 246 = 871
498 + 123 = 621
875 + ...
519 + 283 = 802

Page 10 — Addition — Regrouping Hundreds

643 + 525

1. Add ones. Ask: Do I need to regroup?
2. Add tens. Ask: Do I need to regroup? 643 + 525 = ...8
3. Add hundreds. Ask: Do I need to regroup? 643 + 525 = 1,168

11 hundreds = 1 thousand 1 hundred

Add. Regroup when needed.

942 + 837 = 1,779
564 + 725 = 1,289
473 + 619 = 1,092
620 + 839 = 1,459
385 + 261 = 646
308 + 924 = 1,232

Page 11 — Let's Climb to the Top!

562 + 614 = 1176
921 + 87 = 1008
409 + 736 = 1145
328 + 449 = 777
824 + 597 = 1421
246 + 492 = 738
982 + 220 = 1202
207 + 913 = 1120
547 + 782 = 1329
462 + 781 = 1243
826 + 95 = 921
621 + 489 = 1110
284 + 493 = 777
429 + 636 = 1065
506 + 214 = 720
200 + 489 = 689
684 + 519 = 1203
623 + 192 = 815
536 + 184 = 720
425 + 594 = 1019

Page 12 — Addition — Regrouping Hundreds

12 hundreds = 1 thousand 2 hundreds

526 + 732

1. Add ones: ...8
2. Add tens: 58
3. Add hundreds: 1,258

12 hundreds = 1 thousand 2 hundreds

Wordsearch! Find Crossword puzzle addition is a hoot!

Add. Regroup when needed.

724 + 643 = 1,367
342 + 936 = 1,278
729 + 643 = 1,372
508 + 818 = 1,326
583 + 425 = 1,008
846 + 239 = 1,085

Page 13 — Puzzling Problems

Across
1. 548 + 629 = 1177
6. 387 + 321 = 708? (partial)
12. 912 + 693 = ...
2. 538 + 347 = ...
9. 368 + ...
15. 993 + 795 = ...
3. 381 + 456 = ...
8. 919 + 819 = ...
16. 824 + 423 = ...
4. 536 + 195 = ...
11. 189 + 267 = ...
17. 946 + 238 = ...
5. 265 + 845 = ...
10. 642 + 793 = ...
17. 895 + 909 = ...
5. 963 + 282 = ...
13. 267 + 285 = ...

Down
1. 527 + 681 = ...
7. 248 + 623 = ...
14. 824 + 890 = ...

Page 14 — Four-Digit Addition With Regrouping

10 hundreds = 1 thousand

3428 + 2714

1. Add ones: 2
2. Add tens: 42
3. Add hundreds: 142
4. Add thousands: 6142

Did You Know?
• 1,000 pennies = $10.00!
• 1,000 years is called a millennium!
• 1,000 × 1,000 = 1,000,000 (one million)!
• The Earth rotates on its axis at (about) 1,000 miles per hour!

Add. Regroup when needed.

3415 + 2953 = 6,368
6482 + 1705 = 8,187
5340 + 1828 = 7,168
9426 + 382 = 9,808
2428 + 3197 = 5,625
3456 + 6619 = 10,075

Page 15 — Bubble Math

Add the problems inside these bubbles.

5642 + 1819 = 7461
4629 + 1258 = 5887
2647 + 3281 = 5928
3426 + 2841 = 6267
3690 + 2434 = 6124
4625 + 1817 = 6442
6813 + 2391 = 9204? (8604)
5942 + 1829 = 7771
5642 + 2919 = 8561
2643 + 7427 = 10,070
1923 + 2648 = 4571
4826 + 2098 = 6900? (6924)
2641 + 6259 = 8900
8465 + 1386 = 9851
1805 + 1839 = 9044?
5246 + 3187 = 8433
4269 + 3827 = 8092
9124 + 1348 = 10,472
3142 + 2639 = 5781

These bubbles all popped in order from least to greatest. Number from 1 to 20 the order in which they popped starting with the smallest sum.

Page 16 — Four-Digit Addition With Regrouping

2374 + 3135

1. Add ones: 9
2. Add tens: 09
3. Add hundreds: 509
4. Add thousands: 5509

Add. Regroup when needed.

6208 + 1913 = 8,121
2352 + 1292 = 3,644
5416 + 5298 = 10,714
2671 + 3619 = 6,290
7526 + 2484 = 10,010
3614 + 2902 = 6,516

Math IF5104 — 45 — ©MCMXCIV Instructional Fair, Inc.

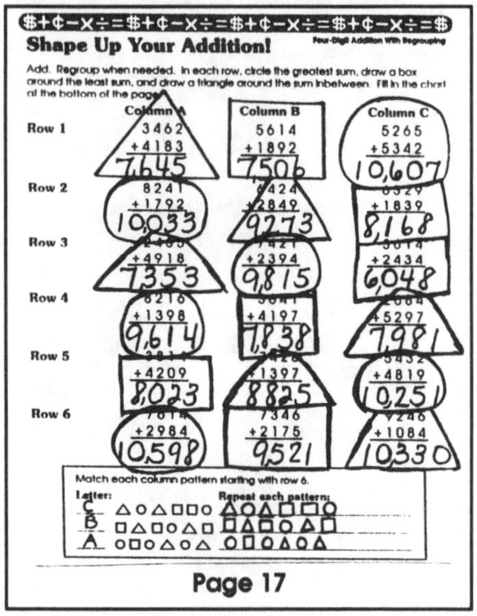

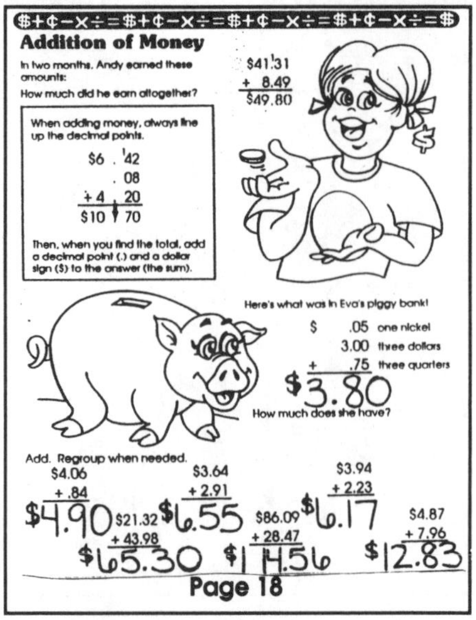

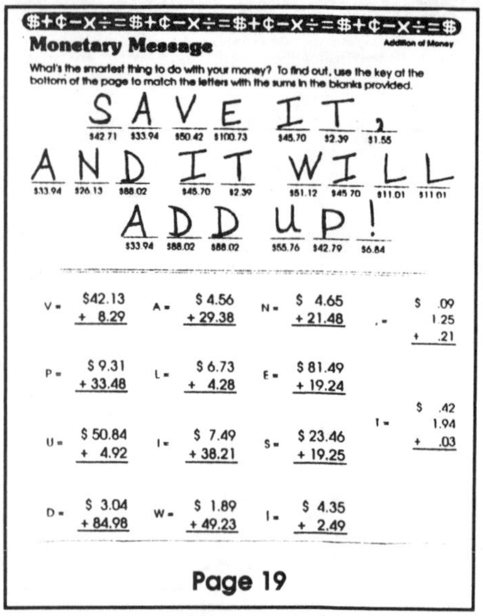

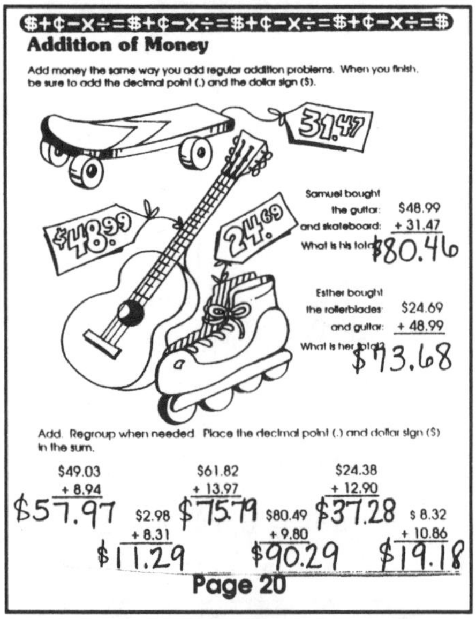

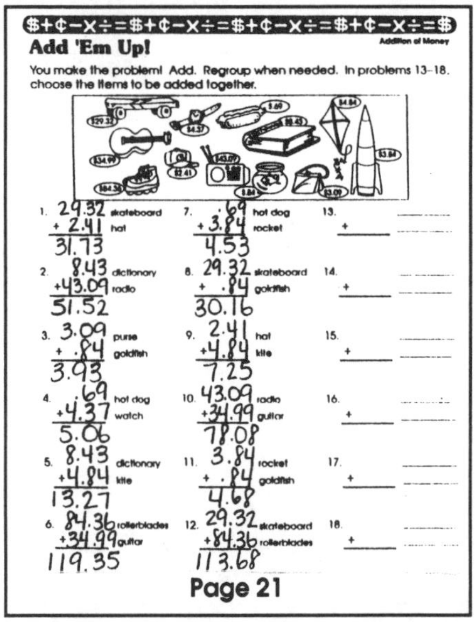

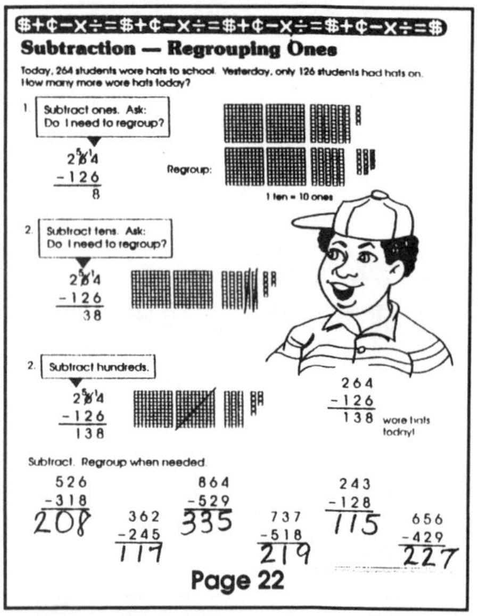

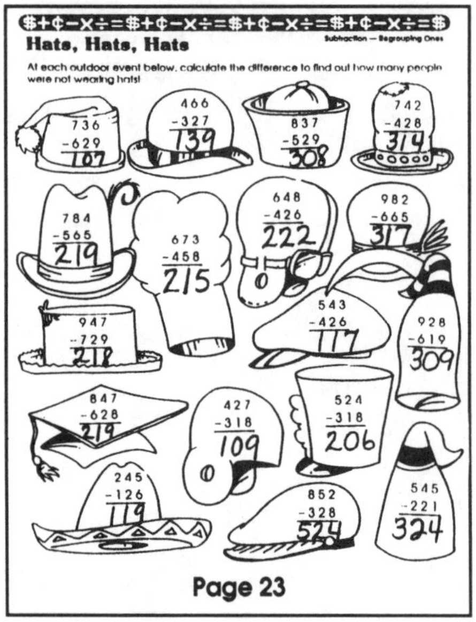

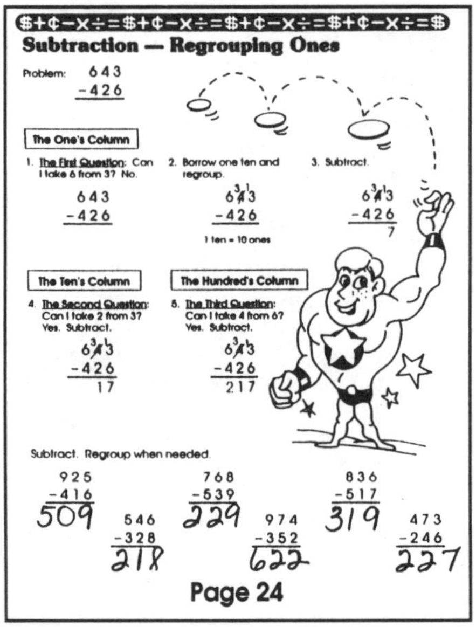

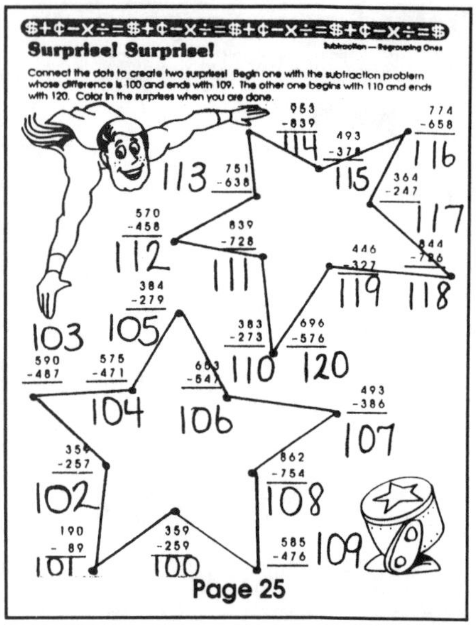

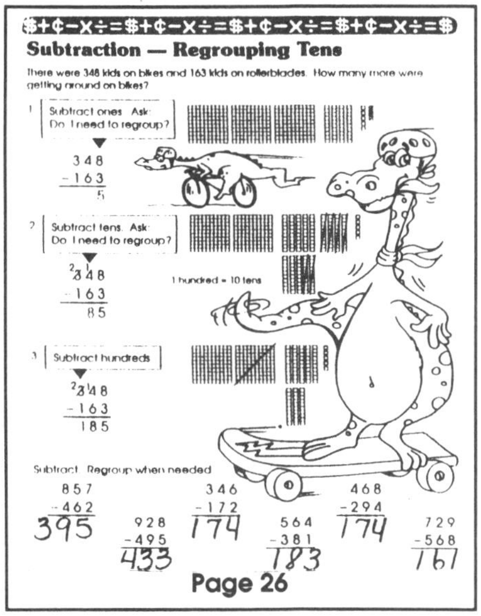
Subtraction — Regrouping Tens

There were 348 kids on bikes and 163 kids on rollerblades. How many more were getting around on bikes?

1. Subtract ones. Ask: Do I need to regroup? 348 − 163 = 5
2. Subtract tens. Ask: Do I need to regroup? 348 − 163 = 85

1 hundred = 10 tens

3. Subtract hundreds. 348 − 163 = 185

Subtract. Regroup when needed.

857 − 462 = 395; 928 − 495 = 433; 346 − 172 = 174; 564 − 381 = 183; 468 − 294 = 174; 729 − 568 = 161

Page 26

Dino-Might

Subtraction — Regrouping Tens

Whenever you're using "kid transportation," what is the best thing to do? To find out, use the key at the bottom of the page to match the letters with the differences in the blanks provided.

ALWAYS WEAR A HELMET!

A = 348 − 153; I = 765 − 673; S = 427 − 382; M = 568 − 475

T = 637 − 446; H = 878 − 697; Y = 548 − 363; W = 748 − 483

E = 824 − 653; R = 439 − 256; L = 447 − 373

Page 27

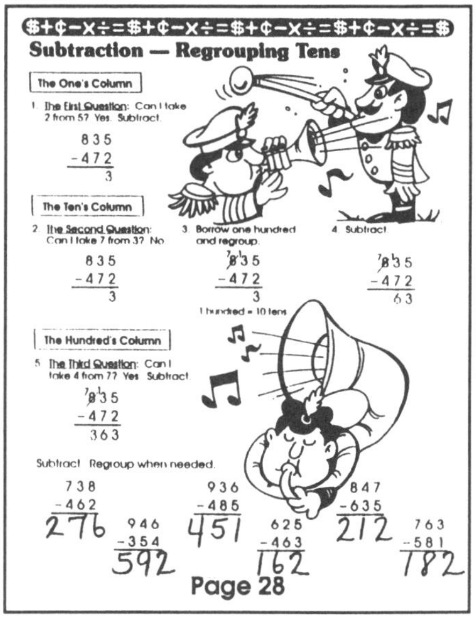
Subtraction — Regrouping Tens

The One's Column

1. The First Question: Can I take 2 from 5? Yes. Subtract. 835 − 472 = 3

The Ten's Column

2. The Second Question: Can I take 7 from 3? No.
3. Borrow one hundred and regroup.
4. Subtract. 835 − 472 = 63

1 hundred = 10 tens

The Hundred's Column

5. The Third Question: Can I take 4 from 7? Yes. Subtract. 835 − 472 = 363

Subtract. Regroup when needed.

738 − 462 = 276; 946 − 354 = 592; 936 − 485 = 451; 625 − 463 = 162; 847 − 635 = 212; 763 − 581 = 182

Page 28

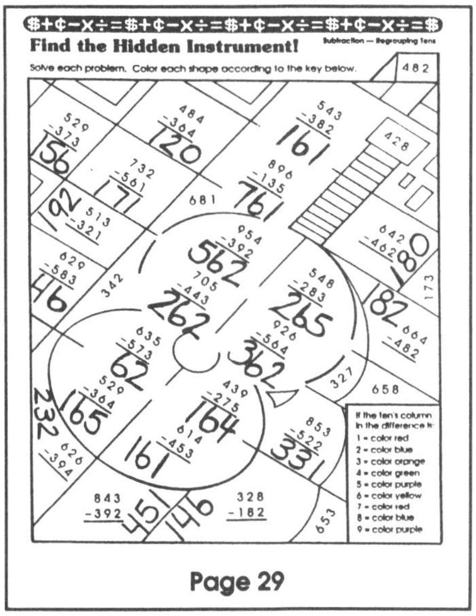
Find the Hidden Instrument!

Subtraction — Regrouping Tens

Solve each problem. Color each shape according to the key below.

529 − 373 = 156; 484 − 364 = 120; 543 − 382 = 161; 732 − 561 = 171; 896 − 135 = 761; 513 − 321 = 192; 954 − 392 = 562; 642 − 462 = 180; 629 − 583 = 46; 705 − 443 = 262; 548 − 283 = 265; 664 − 482 = 182; 635 − 573 = 62; 926 − 564 = 362; 529 − 364 = 165; 439 − 275 = 164; 853 − 522 = 331; 614 − 453 = 161; 626 − 394 = 232; 843 − 392 = 451; 328 − 182 = 146

482, 428, 681, 342, 173, 327, 658, 653

If the ten's column in the difference is: 1 = color red; 2 = color blue; 3 = color orange; 4 = color green; 5 = color purple; 6 = color yellow; 7 = color red; 8 = color blue; 9 = color purple

Page 29

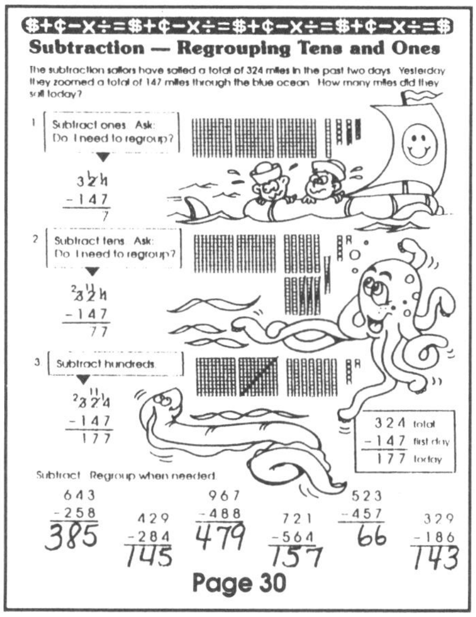
Subtraction — Regrouping Tens and Ones

The subtraction sailors have sailed a total of 324 miles in the past two days. Yesterday they zoomed a total of 147 miles through the blue ocean. How many miles did they sail today?

1. Subtract ones. Ask: Do I need to regroup? 324 − 147 = 7
2. Subtract tens. Ask: Do I need to regroup? 324 − 147 = 77
3. Subtract hundreds. 324 − 147 = 177

324 total − 147 first day = 177 today

Subtract. Regroup when needed.

643 − 258 = 385; 429 − 284 = 145; 967 − 488 = 479; 721 − 564 = 157; 523 − 457 = 66; 329 − 186 = 143

Page 30

Sailing Through Subtraction

Subtraction — Regrouping Tens and Ones

Start at the bottom and work your way up the sails.

542 − 383 = 159; 638 − 453 = 185; 836 − 478 = 358; 737 − 448 = 289

243 − 154 = 89; 567 − 384 = 183; 984 − 643 = 341; 468 − 399 = 69

524 − 342 = 182; 674 − 495 = 179; 374 − 185 = 189; 246 − 158 = 88

852 − 464 = 388; 736 − 557 = 179; 642 − 557 = 85; 435 − 286 = 149

Page 31

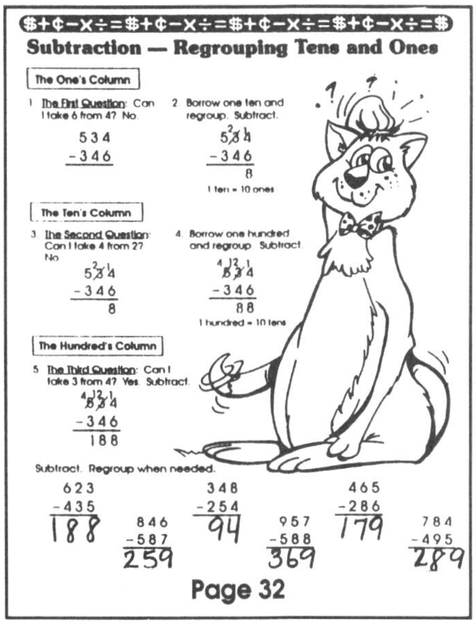
Subtraction — Regrouping Tens and Ones

The One's Column

1. The First Question: Can I take 6 from 4? No. 534 − 346
2. Borrow one ten and regroup. Subtract. 534 − 346 = 8

1 ten = 10 ones

The Ten's Column

3. The Second Question: Can I take 4 from 2? No.
4. Borrow one hundred and regroup. Subtract. 534 − 346 = 88

1 hundred = 10 tens

The Hundred's Column

5. The Third Question: Can I take 3 from 4? Yes. Subtract. 534 − 346 = 188

Subtract. Regroup when needed.

623 − 435 = 188; 846 − 587 = 259; 348 − 254 = 94; 957 − 588 = 369; 465 − 286 = 179; 784 − 495 = 289

Page 32

Secret Salutation

Subtraction — Regrouping Tens and Ones

What is Monica saying to everyone out in Subtractionland? To find out, use the key at the bottom of the page to match the letters with the differences in the blanks provided.

HI, BOYS AND GIRLS!

Key:

O = 524 − 136; D = 518 − 239; H = 324 − 268; I = 624 − 168

I = 846 − 397; G = 642 − 284; B = 418 − 169; ! = 916 − 238

S = 427 − 149; R = 825 − 246; , = 821 − 346

N = 234 − 96; Y = 521 − 246; A = 467 − 179

Page 33

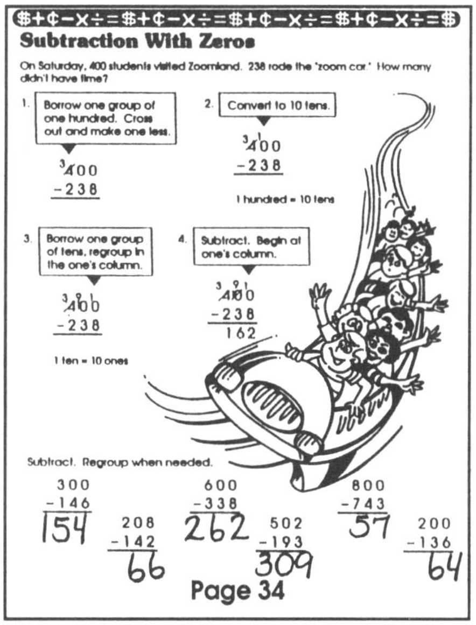
Subtraction With Zeros

On Saturday, 400 students visited Zoomland. 238 rode the "zoom car." How many didn't have time?

1. Borrow one group of one hundred. Cross out and make one less. 400 − 238
2. Convert to 10 tens. 400 − 238

1 hundred = 10 tens

3. Borrow one group of tens, regroup in the one's column. 400 − 238

1 ten = 10 ones

4. Subtract. Begin at one's column. 400 − 238 = 162

Subtract. Regroup when needed.

300 − 146 = 154; 208 − 142 = 66; 600 − 338 = 262; 502 − 193 = 309; 800 − 743 = 57; 200 − 136 = 64

Page 34

Round and Round She Goes . . . — Subtraction With Zeros

Take a ride completely around this Ferris wheel subtracting with zeros.

800 − 736 = 64; 406 − 243 = 163; 200 − 82 = 118; 800 − 746 = 54; 600 − 432 = 168; 500 − 248 = 252; 300 − 284 = 16; 400 − 365 = 35; 900 − 824 = 76; 400 − 278 = 122; 700 − 543 = 157; 900 − 623 = 277

Page 35

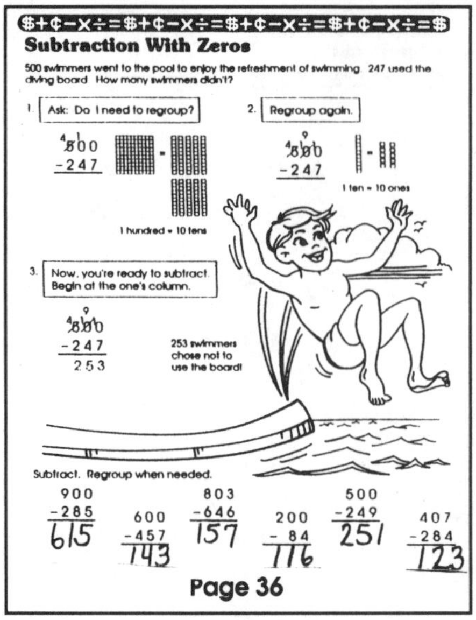
Subtraction With Zeros

500 swimmers went to the pool to enjoy the refreshment of swimming. 247 used the diving board. How many swimmers didn't?

1. Ask: Do I need to regroup? 500 − 247; 1 hundred = 10 tens
2. Regroup again. 500 − 247; 1 ten = 10 ones
3. Now, you're ready to subtract. Begin at the one's column. 500 − 247 = 253. 253 swimmers chose not to use the board!

Subtract. Regroup when needed.

900 − 285 = 615; 600 − 457 = 143; 803 − 646 = 157; 200 − 84 = 116; 500 − 249 = 251; 407 − 284 = 123

Page 36

Dive Into Subtraction! — Subtraction With Zeros

Complete the puzzle by solving the problems below.

Across: 1. 600 − 247; 4. 800 − 145; 6. 800 − 527; 7. 200 − 172; 8. 807 − 142; 9. 904 − 285; 11. 600 − 427; 12. 903 − 624; 13. 900 − 264; 15. 800 − 386; 17. 800 − 527

Down: 2. 700 − 184; 3. 900 − 448; 5. 900 − 764; 7. 500 − 243; 10. 400 − 248; 11. 500 − 304; 14. 800 − 138; 15. 708 − 269; 16. 900 − 468

Page 37

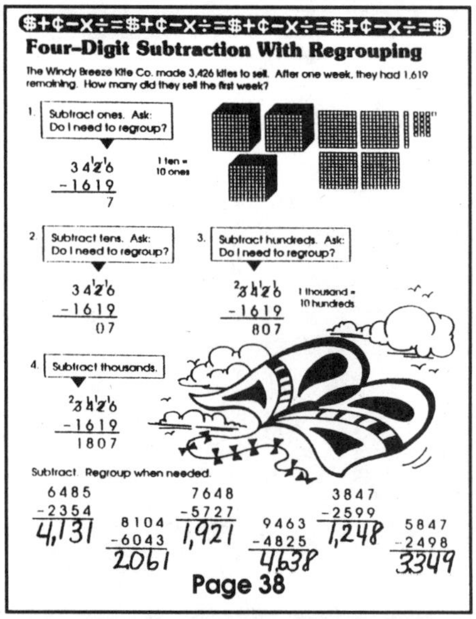
Four-Digit Subtraction With Regrouping

The Windy Breeze Kite Co. made 3,426 kites to sell. After one week, they had 1,619 remaining. How many did they sell the first week?

1. Subtract ones. Ask: Do I need to regroup? 3426 − 1619 → 7 (1 ten = 10 ones)
2. Subtract tens. Ask: Do I need to regroup? → 07
3. Subtract hundreds. Ask: Do I need to regroup? → 807 (1 thousand = 10 hundreds)
4. Subtract thousands. → 1807

Subtract. Regroup when needed.

6485 − 2354 = 4,131; 8104 − 6043 = 2061; 7648 − 5727 = 1,921; 9463 − 4825 = 4638; 3847 − 2599 = 1,248; 5847 − 2498 = 3349

Page 38

Kite Craze! — Four-Digit Subtraction With Regrouping

Subtract. How will you get way up there to solve the problems?

8794 − 6428 = 2366; 9643 − 8825 = 818; 8825 − 7436 = 1389; 5648 − 3929 = 1719; 7006 − 6223 = 783; 8416 − 3509 = 4907; 4162 − 2840 = 1322; 6514 − 3282 = 3232; 5436 − 2924 = 2512; 9246 − 8518 = 728; 4862 − 3946 = 916; 9486 − 6294 = 3192; 9085 − 6241 = 2844; 8462 − 6391 = 2071; 7643 − 6521 = 1122; 6430 − 4252 = 2178

Page 39

Four-Digit Subtraction With Regrouping

The One's Column
1. The First Question: Can I take 5 from 4? No. 8294 − 2635
2. Borrow one ten and regroup. Subtract. (1 ten = 10 ones) → 9

The Ten's Column
3. The Second Question: Can I take 3 from 8? Yes. Subtract. → 59

The Hundred's Column
4. The Third Question: Can I take 6 from 2? No. → 59
5. Borrow one thousand and regroup. Subtract. (1 thousand = 10 hundreds) → 659

The Thousand's Column
6. The Third Question: Can I take 2 from 7? Yes. Subtract. → 5659

Subtract. Regroup when needed.

5642 − 1821 = 3,821; 8923 − 1364 = 7,559; 8409 − 1182 = 7,227; 4628 − 1714 = 2,914; 7562 − 1681 = 5,881; 4238 − 1449 = 2,789

Page 40

Subtraction on Stage! — Four-Digit Subtraction With Regrouping

These subtraction problems are heading west. Solve 'em. It'll be a bouncy ride. Just hold on!

5648 − 2425 = 3,223; 2148 − 825 = 1,323; 7641 − 5246 = 2,395; 7648 − 3289 = 4,359; 5408 − 1291 = 4,117; 8209 − 4182 = 4,027; 8419 − 2182 = 6,237; 6249 − 1526 = 4,723; 6428 − 4159 = 2269; 4287 − 2492 = 1,795; 7645 − 2826 = 4819; 2016 − 1021 = 995; 7689 − 2845 = 4844; 8247 − 6459 = 1,788; 9047 − 6152 = 2895; 5231 − 1642 = 3,589

Page 41

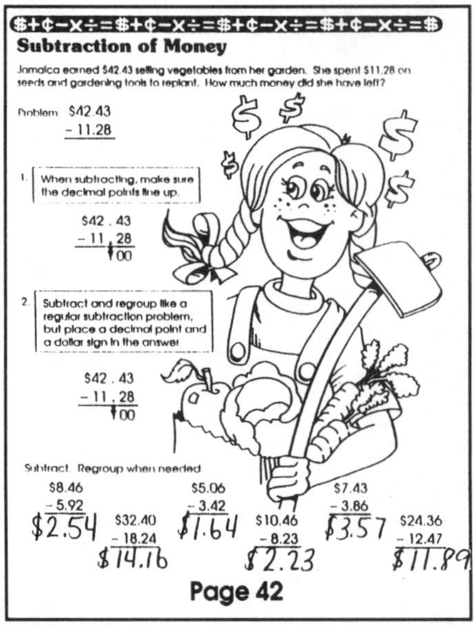
Subtraction of Money

Jamaica earned $42.43 selling vegetables from her garden. She spent $11.28 on seeds and gardening tools to replant. How much money did she have left?

Problem: $42.43 − 11.28

1. When subtracting, make sure the decimal points line up. $42.43 − 11.28 → 00
2. Subtract and regroup like a regular subtraction problem, but place a decimal point and a dollar sign in the answer. $42.43 − 11.28 → 00

Subtract. Regroup when needed.

$8.46 − 5.92 = $2.54; $32.40 − 18.24 = $14.16; $5.06 − 3.42 = $1.64; $10.46 − 8.23 = $2.23; $7.43 − 3.86 = $3.57; $24.36 − 12.47 = $11.89

Page 42

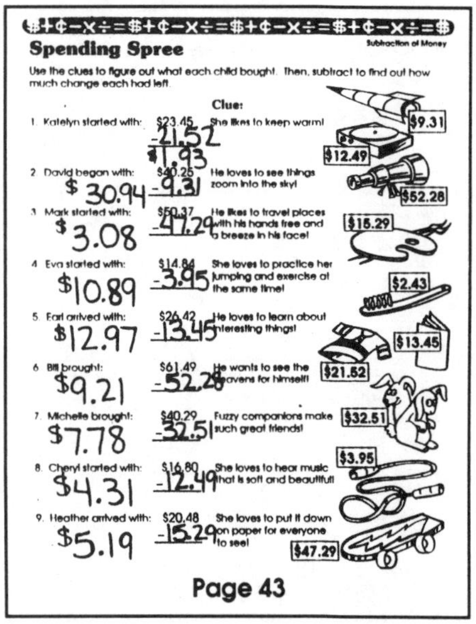
Spending Spree — Subtraction of Money

Use the clues to figure out what each child bought. Then, subtract to find out how much change each had left.

Clue:

1. Katelyn started with: $23.45 − 21.52 = $1.93 — She likes to keep warm!
2. David began with: $40.25 − 9.31 = $30.94 — He loves to see things zoom into the sky!
3. Mark started with: $50.37 − 47.29 = $3.08 — He likes to travel places with his hands free and a breeze in his face!
4. Eva started with: $14.84 − 3.95 = $10.89 — She loves to practice her jumping and exercise at the same time!
5. Earl arrived with: $26.42 − 13.45 = $12.97 — He loves to learn about interesting things!
6. Bill brought: $61.49 − 52.28 = $9.21 — He wants to see the heavens for himself!
7. Michelle brought: $40.29 − 32.51 = $7.78 — Fuzzy companions make such great friends!
8. Cheryl started with: $16.80 − 12.49 = $4.31 — She loves to hear music that is soft and beautiful!
9. Heather arrived with: $20.48 − 15.29 = $5.19 — She loves to put it down on paper for everyone to see!

$9.31, $12.49, $52.28, $15.29, $2.43, $13.45, $21.52, $32.51, $3.95, $47.29

Page 43